IN PURSUIT OF GOLD

LAPIDUS

In Pursuit
of Gold

Alchemy in
Theory and Practice

Additions and Extractions by
STEPHEN SKINNER

NEW YORK

SAMUEL WEISER

1976

First published in the United States in 1976 by
SAMUEL WEISER, INC.
734 Broadway, New York, N.Y. 10003
© Lapidus 1976
ISBN 0 87728 360 5

MANUFACTURED IN GREAT BRITAIN

Contents

Nature

Hidden deep in the heart of things,
Thou carest for growth and life.
The seed becomes shoot, the bud a blossom,
the flower becomes fruit.
Tired I slept on my idle bed
in the illusion that the work had an end.
In the morning I awoke to find
That my garden was full of flowers.

Rabindranath Tagore

Miracles are not contrary to nature,
but only contrary to what we know about nature.

St. Augustine, A.D. 353

Illustrations

The pictures displayed in this book are taken from an illustrated treatise by Michael Maier, an artist in alchemy, published in 1618, under the title *Atalanta Fugiens*, and printed in Latin. There are fifty beautiful copper engravings, showing much detail, which are symbolic pictures of the different aspects of the art of alchemy, that are said to be "accommodated partly to the eyes, and partly to the understanding".

Only a few of these plates, the most helpful, have been introduced here. In the original work, the pictures are not in any special order, therefore a few guiding remarks have been added under each picture, by the present author, which may make them more useful to the interested student.

These pictures, it must be remembered, are nothing more than the fanciful imaginations of an artistic author whose intention was to simultaneously reveal and conceal the secrets of alchemy. Indeed, such mixed intentions are quite a common thing in alchemical literature.

Introduction

Owing to the disparagement cast on the art of alchemy in modern times by those who have failed to unearth its secrets, it has been by-passed by science, and has become obscured to the point where few people even clearly understand what it stands for. If asked what is alchemy, the short answer might be the search for the "Philosophers' Stone". This, however, is no stone, but a powder with the power to transmute base metals into gold or silver.

Thousands of books have been written on the subject throughout the centuries, in many languages and in many parts of the world. It may possibly be conjectured that this is how the unfortunate Incas of Peru produced such great quantities of gold; or again it may be hazarded that from the same source came the gold with which King Solomon decorated his temple so lavishly in biblical times.

The "Philosophers' Stone" was also called the *"Elixir of Life"*, which has the virtue of being able to cure any of the diseases of mankind, thus assuring perfect health and a longevity far beyond the normal span that is hoped for by man.

Artephius, an alchemist of the twelfth century, wrote in his treatise entitled *The Secret Book* that up to that time he had already lived a thousand years by aid of the Elixir. Among others famed for longevity in more modern times, there was the mysterious Count de St. Germain, who never appeared to grow older in appearance. In the seventeenth century, King Frederick the Great named him, "the man who does not die". These men were always known to flit from one country to another to preserve their identity and conceal their secret, to prevent their lives from being endangered.

Why, in spite of so much literature on alchemy, are we still in the dark with regard to its processes? The simple answer is that there is hardly a treatise among the many thousands that can be clearly understood. The men who wrote them were always in fear of the dangers that would inevitably follow anyone rash enough to expose his knowledge too frankly. Human greed has always been a deterrent against open declarations of success in the art, and therefore the philosophers thought it best either to remain silent, which many did, or else record their knowledge in the curious symbolic forms which each decided for himself; and what a chaos and babel has ensued from all these treatises! It is from such writings that today we derive the word "gibberish", coming as it does from works by the eighth-century Arabian adept known as Geber, who wrote the truth in a fashion that few can follow.

Because of this confusion, alchemy will not lightly open her doors to the dilettante. The treatises are full of stumbling blocks, blinds, misleading statements, important keys left out and lies put in: many names are given to one thing and one name given to many things. There are also many books written by ignorant rogues who battened on greedy rich men to trick the money out of their coffers.

It is important to remember that, if alchemy is a true science, and an art mastered by men of past ages, who were simple-minded by comparison with present knowledge and standards of research, how much easier ought it to be today to uncover all their secrets with our resources, equipment and materials. However there must be some prior belief in the feasibility of attaining the goal sought, for without this, one could not persevere undaunted. Although admittedly not easy to discover, many adepts in alchemy wrote that the art was really quite easy and, when once known, "child's play and woman's work". One cannot help arriving at the conclusion that the very simplicity of the work may have been the chief cause of the failure of so many brilliant workers in this field. Among the secrets that were lacking was the knowledge of the correct timing and heating techniques.

It is worthwhile to again attempt the unravelling of this great problem. In many ways we today have many advantages and facilities which they sorely lacked. For example, their fairly primitive furnaces which were heated with charcoal, wood, and less savoury fuels, were difficult to control at a constant temperature over long periods of time, whereas our modern thermostatically controlled hot-plates are able to carry on this task continuously without some-one constantly in attendance. Again, the measurement of tempera-tures was another difficulty as the men of old depended upon feeling with their hands or using hot sand, water baths and such like; all of which means nothing to us in these days of thermometers and thermostats.

Modern science has not yet reached the state of all knowledge, and those secrets of nature that are known are indeed still a very minute part of the whole. In the long-lived family of metals there are still many potential secrets, undreamed of by man, remaining to be discovered. It is therefore unwise, to say the least, to deny the basis for this lost art, because the road to it has not yet been systematically investigated.

Many godfearing men, who had nothing to gain by deception, testified on their death-beds to the truth of alchemy. Moreover, they confirmed that they had completed the work more than once themselves and furthermore that anyone could do it, at any time and anywhere, at very little cost. They also wrote that, because of its simplicity, fools would ridicule the art, were the materials and processes to become known. They concealed what they knew, so that alchemy should not become common property. Thus, for the present the secrets are concealed, but not irretrievably lost. It is the intention of this book to raise the aura of complexity from alchemical writings, and once again restore the interest of enterprising minds in the subject.

It is proposed to examine only a few treatises, those which are the most lucid, sincere and genuine. Every endeavour will be made to explain and illuminate these writings, most of which are very rare (although some have been reprinted, and the rest may still be found in the British Museum Library). They were written often in Latin by masters who asserted they had themselves completed the work. Other less helpful works will be ignored to avoid confusing the student.

It is generally imagined by those who are rather vague about the subject that alchemy has some connection with occultism, yoga or witchcraft, and possibly magical practices; and booksellers quite often group alchemical books with these subjects together on their bookshelves. This idea is altogether erroneous. Alchemy has no connection whatsoever with these matters except that their practitioners sometimes also pursued alchemy. To suppose this is to make nonsense of all alchemical writings, for it is a purely chemical knowledge. Indeed, what has salt, sulphur and mercury, the three principles of the art, to do with religion or spiritual thought? It is

13

well known that the art has been equated with religious or psychological ideas by some people who have failed to understand the treatises, and still persist in trying to read these meanings into the writings.

"Our principles know it is but one, and that is in metals. Even those metals which you may buy commonly, the best of them; you must be a master and not just a scholar, namely as it is wisely said in *Norton*: 'To know how to destroy their whole composition, that some of their components may help in the conclusion'."

Take good notice of what was said by Norton in 1678 in the above quotation from *Ripley Revived*. During past ages everything under the sun has been tried out by ignoramuses in their attempts to produce the Philosophers' Stone. Again, from the above-mentioned book, to emphasise the obvious:

"This is according to nature, and it is the true ground of all generation, for out of kind, nothing doth engender; a man begetteth a man, not a lion; nor doth a lion beget a sheep; a rose does not beget a thorn, nor a nettle a gilliflower; and so if need be, I could particularly demonstrate it throughout all vegetables, minerals, and animal bodies; but it is so plain a thing, that I need say no more, and leave it as the foundation stone on which you shall build whatever you intend."

Several metals are mentioned in alchemical works, with a number of names attached to them, planetary and otherwise, of which the planetary were in most common use. Here they are given so that they may be recognised later on.

Gold	Sol, sun, the greater luminary, the king.
Silver	Moon, luna, the lesser luminary, the queen.
Copper	Venus.
Lead	Saturn.
Tin	Jupiter.
Iron	Mars.
Mercury	Quicksilver, metalline water.

There is one other metal which is not very common and which will be discussed later in this book, namely Antimony.

That which has been outlined in this introduction has been beautifully summed up in the opening paragraph to the treatise attributed to Hermes entitled *The Golden Tract* included in the composite book known as the *Hermetic Museum* first published in 1678.

"Ancient as well as modern philosophers, most beloved reader, and devoted seeker after true wisdom, when through the Grace of God they reached the goal of their desires, have endeavoured to make their discovery known to their fellow inquirers in all parts of the world—not only because they wished to inform them that the thrice great and good God had enlightened their minds, blessed the labour of their hands, and shown to them the greatest and most profound secret of earthly wisdom (for which benefit all praise, honour and glory are justly due to Him) but also that they might afford assistance to beginners in the art, by which they too might attain to the knowledge of this most holy mystery. Such men there have been in all countries; among the Egyptians, Hermes Trismegistus holds the highest place; then come Chaldeans, Greeks, Arabs, Italians, Gauls, Englishmen, Dutchmen, Spaniards, Germans, Poles, Hungarians, Hebrews and many others. Though the aforementioned sages wrote in different times, and in different languages, yet their works exhibit so marvellous an agreement, that any true philosopher may easily see that all their hearts have been gladdened by God in the discovery of this stone, and that they all had performed this work with their own hands. Now, as the truth of their views is perceived by their agreement, so the disagreement of certain others marks them as false philosophers. For not knowing the foundation of this glorious art, and making up fanciful theories out of their own minds, they exhibit their ignorance to all".

1. The Confusion of Alchemy

So much has been written about alchemy during past centuries that everything possible that could have been said about the subject has been reiterated again and again in a multitude of ways. Therefore it is not surprising that this has resulted in the complete secret art being exposed many times over, although of course never in any one treatise. In fact, some adepts in alchemy have written so many treatises that, from these alone, one may gather the whole secret if their works are properly pieced together in an orderly fashion. But only with experiment may one find enough clues in one author's writings to build up a complete picture, cast out the blinds and pitfalls, and realise that, after all, the art is not so difficult. Although spread chaotically over thousands of volumes, it will indeed emerge that in one page only in a book, the whole theory and practice of the art of alchemy could lie revealed.

Notwithstanding, the reader is warned against haphazard reading of alchemical books, for this will lead to mental confusion, and finally desperation of ever learning anything. Once started on alchemical research however, this becomes a great temptation and a bad fault. One tends to read voraciously any alchemical book that comes to hand. This one book, closely studied, is however all that is necessary for practical experiment.

Every treatise on alchemy is so artfully written that at every reading a different conception arises in the mind: what seemed so clear and helpful yesterday will seem an utter misconception tomorrow and thus it often transpires that a correct understanding is replaced by an error. A well-known modern scientist who had actually written books on alchemy which were mainly quotations and commentary, albeit in fragmentary form, when asked by the present author why he had not experimented himself, sadly remarked, "If I only knew what materials to take in hand to commence with, I would gladly do so." The books by this author are now on library shelves along with many others, all filled with quotations and commentary which lead the readers nowhere, since the modern authors know nothing of practical alchemy.

The metallurgist's outlook on metals differs greatly from the alchemist's view. The latter looks upon metals as living things while they are still unmade into some permanent form, in just the same manner as a farmer will look upon corn before it is made into bread. Both contain the *seed* of growth. Under varying conditions, this seed can be transformed by nature, or it may fail, but it is *always* nature that does this work. The farmer knows the differing conditions by which plants may be made to multiply, and the alchemist likewise must know what treatment the metals demand from nature to give forth their special and characteristic result, and the virtues of the right metal needed to produce the Philosophers' Stone. Although the techniques of the old masters of alchemical science were not quite up to the standard of today's scientists, they were aware of many secrets that for the present are completely lost. Even so modern chemistry has much for which to thank them.

Now to properly understand how the alchemist's mind worked, it is necessary to know that he believed that metals have a life of their own, equal to animals and vegetables. This being so, since in every department of nature there is a constant progression of birth, growth and increase, this natural evolutionary law applies to metals as well. Otherwise one may ask quite logically, why should nature stop at metals? Alchemists maintain that nature does not stop at metals. This fact is not immediately obvious owing to the shortness of human life compared to the long stretches of time necessary for minerals to gestate and develop imperceptibly those changes in nature which occur whilst they are in the earth.

The alchemist constantly reiterates the expression that what takes nature a thousand years, he can bring about in a very short time. Following from this alchemical axiom was the idea that everything living consisted of earth and water. Fire and air were the two other elements which made up their four elements, but these latter two we can ignore for the moment.

Metals, they stated, were made from earth and water, but this water was a "dry water, which did not wet the hand". We must take good notice of this claim, for here lies one of the main stumbling blocks. Here you are presented with the first great secret and problem. Their dry water was not water so much as the vapour given off by metals and, this being hard to come by, was a secret so deeply hidden that men spent their whole lives experimenting without ever discovering it.

The first work of the alchemist was to reduce the solids into liquid or water and, again, the water into solids. "Dissolve and coagulate" was the old axiom of alchemical practice. The solids became a slime, or liquid, and the slime or liquid was thickened into solids again. Thus the artificer dissolved and congealed or coagulated, and mixed the atoms of various principles into one neutral matter, or third thing rarely mentioned, and when mentioned it was called mercury. This mercury disarmed everyone who thought it was just ordinary mercury.

All this work was carried out in a natural manner; no fires or furnaces like the metallurgist uses. The masters said of fire that it kills the life in metals—even as corn made into bread is not fit for planting in the earth to grow again.

One point now must finally be made clear; alchemy does not mean the art of making gold or silver, or precious stones for that matter, since these latter are also possible by the same processes, for man cannot make or create anything that is nature's work. What man may do, provided he has the requisite knowledge, is to change things from one form into another, but not out of their genus, which is quite a different matter. To make this clearer, it may be trite to say that man cannot make a tree, yet he may grow one from seed—but this seed must first be found and planted in the correct manner, in a place and condition suitable to nature's demands. Likewise, he can only produce gold and silver by transmuting other metals into these, and the "know-how" is known as alchemy.

As for the Elixir of Life, conferring immortality is the prerogative of God alone, but to quote from an old book:

> "By virtue of this quintessence, Artephius testifieth that he lived above a thousand years; Flamel also recordeth it, that it triumptheth over all the miseries of the world, Laznioro is more bold, and saith, that if in the agonies of death, a man should taste but a grain of it, all mortal pestilence would depart from him."

As already pointed out, the first difficulty to be met with in alchemical writings has always been the multiplicity of names for

19

most items, purposely invented to mislead. Conversely many different things are called by the same name; for example, as soon as one approaches the art, promptly the name "Mercury" appears. One finds it a prominent term in all the literature on alchemy. This mercury has been permutated and juggled with in a thousand different treatises. They have called it a dry water, which will not wet the hand, and a metalline water, which can destroy metals, and mixes with them all in varying degrees. As is generally known, these facts can be said about ordinary mercury or quicksilver, yet to all the adepts in the art this latter is disdained and is not used. Their mercury, they warn, must be prepared and is permanently fixed, not to be separated from any metal once it is joined to it. Ordinary or vulgar mercury, as they term it, will however volatilise or run out of amalgams when heat is applied. Thus we must conclude that although vulgar mercury fits their description perfectly, yet it would be an error to use this. This problem will be dealt with later in this book. Besides a number of other types of "mercury", many of which will in time give a hint as to what their mercury really is, are mentioned in the following quotations so that the tyro coming across them will be familiarised with the various usages of the word.

They say it is a metal, water, vinegar; at different times, blood and blood red, milk and milky white like cream, silvery, clear, or opaque. Were they being deliberately misleading, or were all these descriptions the truth? No wonder their child's play became a great mystery! In fact, each of these names could describe what the matter in the flask appeared like during the processes that took place at various stages of the alchemical process. *The Secret Book* by Artephius presented later in this book will help solve this difficulty to a great extent.

There is another important item of which to take note. When the alchemists speak of "Our Gold" or "Our Mercury" or "Philosopher's Mercury", they are really speaking of metals that they have processed as, for example, corn made into flour, might be termed "Our Corn", thus indicating that the item referred to was not in its original state.

If all this seems complicated, the reader may be assured that it is not so; patience and perseverence are all that are needed and everything will fall into place and become clear. Skimming over anything, or turning to the end pages will not help at all, for like any other science, alchemy demands careful study, and a careful grasp of what is explained. These preliminary explanations will later make everything clearer, and the determined alchemist will save many long years of wasteful experiments, and money.

Before drawing too near to those treatises whose importance consists in seeming plainly written, with apparently full instructions both in theory and practice, we would like to present the explanatory treatise by Philalethes entitled *A Brief Guide to the Celestial Ruby*. It may further help the reader to grasp the import of what follows in the rest of the book. This work is also abridged. *A Brief Guide* is one of many treatises to be found in the *Hermetic Museum* published in 1678 in two volumes. It may be of interest to know that these two volumes have been republished in facsimile in 1893, 1953 and 1973; and there the reader will find the treatise in full.

A BRIEF GUIDE TO THE CELESTIAL RUBY
by Eirenæus Philalethes

"The Philosophers' Stone is a certain heavenly, spiritual, penetrative, and fixed substance, which brings all metals to the perfection of gold and silver, and that by natural methods, which yet in their effects transcend nature.

"It is prepared from one substance, of which the art of chemistry is conversant, to which nothing is added, and from which nothing is taken away, except that its superfluities are removed. [The superfluities are a useless sediment.]

"No one will question the utility of our art, if he believes that it enables us to transmute base metals into gold. That base metals are capable of such transmutation, is clear; nature has destined them all to become gold, but they have not been properly matured. If then that which hinders their perfect digestion be removed, they will all become gold; for crude, cold, and moist mercury is the common first substance of gold as well as of other metals. Hence all other metals may be perfected into gold by the aid of

21

our art, which being projected upon imperfect metals, has power to quicken the maturing process by as much as itself exceeds the standard maturity of gold. How potent then must be the spiritual nature of our stone, which can effect more in one hour by a bare projection than nature in the course of the ages.

"If that substance which nature supplies be taken in hand by art, dissolved, coagulated and digested, its perfection is increased from a monadic to a denary virtue; by repeating the same process, it is increased a hundred-fold, and then a thousand-fold, etc. This wonderful medicine penetrates each smallest part of the base metal in proportion of 1 to 1000, and tinges them through and through with its noble nature. A reproach is sometimes levelled at our art, as though it claimed the power of creating gold; every attentive reader will know that it only arrogates to itself the power of developing through the removal of all defects and superfluities, the golden nature, which the baser metals possess in common with that highly digested metalline substance.

"Those foolish people who seek for the substance of our stone outside the domain of metals will never arrive at any satisfactory conclusion. For as a lion is always born of a lion and a man of a man, so all things owe their birth to that which they are like. Thus you see that the stone which is to be the transformer of metals into gold must be sought in the precious metals, in which it is enclosed and contained. It is called a stone by virtue of its fixed nature, and it resists the action of the fire as successfully as any stone. In species, it is gold, more pure than the purest; it is fixed and incombustible like a stone, but its appearance is that of a very fine powder, impalpable to the touch, fragment as to smell, in potency a most penetrative spirit, apparently dry, and yet unctuous, and easily capable of tingeing a plate of metal.

"How is this stone to be obtained? It does not exist in nature, but has to be prepared by art, in obedience to nature's law. Its substance is in metals, but in form it differs widely from them; and in this sense, the metals are not our stone. It is necessary then to reduce metallic bodies to their homogeneous water which does not wet the hands, and that from this water there may be generated a new metallic species, which is nobler by far than any existing metal, viz., our Celestial Ruby.

"The whole process which we employ closely resembles that

followed by nature in the bowels of the earth, except that it is much shorter. Nature produces the metals out of cold and humid mercury, and by assiduous digestion; our art takes the same crude and humid mercury, and conjoins it with mature gold, by a secret artifice; the mixture represents a new and far more potent mercury which by digestion, becomes not common gold, but one more noble, which can transmute imperfect metals into pure gold.

"Thus you see though our stone is made of gold alone, yet it is not common gold; the latter must be dissolved in our mineral water which does not wet the hands; this water is mercury, extracted from the red servant, and is capable of accomplishing our work without any further trouble. It is the one true natural first substance, to which nothing is added, and from which nothing is subtracted, except certain superfluities, which however it will cast off without any aid by its own inherent vital action.

"Consider these signs, that which dissolves is spirit; that which coagulates is body. A body cannot enter a body so as to cause dissolution, but a spirit can enter it, attenuate, and clarify it. For every agent has a tendency to assimilate to itself that which it acts upon, and every natural effect is conformed to the nature of the efficient; hence water is necessary if you would extract water from earth.

"When I speak of water, I do not mean aquafortis, or any other corrosive whatsoever, for these waters, instead of dissolving metal only corrode, mar, and corrupt them, without destroying their old form to which task they are insufficient, as they are not of a metallic nature. No, our water is the water of mercury, which dissolves homogeneous metallic bodies, and mingles with them in indissoluble union, abides with them, is digested with them, and together with them become the spiritual whole which we seek. For everything which dissolves a substance naturally, still preserving the specific properties of the thing dissolved, becomes one with it, coalesces with it, and is thickened by it, thus nourishing it; as we see in the case of a grain of wheat, which when dissolved by the humid earthy vapour, thereby takes up that vapour as its radical moisture, and grows together with it into a plant.

"Common gold, if mixed with common mercury, or anything except its own essential, is not dissolved, because such waters are too crude, cold and impure; for which reason, being utterly unlike

23

gold, they cannot amalgamate with it, or attain with it to a far nobler degree of development. Our mercury, indeed, is cold and unmatured, in comparison with gold, but it is pure hot and well digested in respect of common mercury, which resembles it only in whiteness and fluxibility. Our mercury is in fact a pure water, clean, clear, bright, and resplendent, worthy of all admiration.

"Our stone is produced from one thing, and four mercurial substances, of which one is mature; the others pure but crude, two of them being extracted in a wonderful manner from their ore by means of the third. The four are amalgamated by the intervention of a gentle fire, and there subjected to conction day by day, until all become one by natural, and not manual conjunction.

"Afterwards the fire being changed, these volatile substances should be fixed and digested by means of heat which becomes a little more powerful every day, (i.e., by means of fixed and incombustible sulphur of the same genus) until the whole compound attains to the same essence, fixity and colour.

"There are many degrees or phases of this our process, which I may describe as follows. The first is calcination. Calcination is the first purgation of the stone, the drying up of its humours, through its natural heat, which is stirred into vital action by the eternal heat of water, whereby the compound is converted into a black powder, which is yet unctuous and retains its radical humour. This calcination is performed for the purpose of rendering the substance viscous, spongy, and more especially penetratable; for gold in itself is highly fixed, and difficult of solution even in our water, but through this calcination, it becomes soft and white, and we observe it in its two natures, the fixed and the volatile, which we liken to two serpents. In order that a full dissolution may be made, there is need of contrition, that the calcination may afterwards produce a viscous state, when it will be fit for dissolution.

"When the substances are first mixed, they are at enmity with each other, by reason of their contrary qualities, for there is the heat and dryness of the sulphur fiercely contending with the cold and moisture of the mercury. They can only be reconciled in a medium which partakes of both natures, and the medium in which heat and cold are reconciled is dryness which can co-exist with both. Thus cold and heat are brought to dwell peaceably together

24

in the dryness of the earth, and the dryness and the moisture in the coldness of the water.

"Its sufficient cause is the action of the inward heat upon the moisture, whereby everything that resists it is converted into a very fine powder; the moving and instrumental cause is the fire contrary to nature, which being hidden in our solvent water, battles with its moisture, and digests it into a viscous or unctuous powder.

"Calcination then is the beginning of the work, and without it there can be neither peaceable commixtion, nor proper union. The first dealbation reduces the substance to its two principles, sulphur and mercury; the first of which is fixed, while the other is volatile. They are compared to two serpents, the fixed substance to a serpent without wings, and the volatile substance to a serpent with wings. One serpent holds in his mouth the tail of the other, to show that they are indissolubly conjoined by community of birth and destiny, and that our art is accomplished by the joint working of this mercurial sulphur, and sulphureous mercury. Hence the whole compound is at this stage called 'Rebis', because they are two substances, but only one essence. They are not really two, but one and the same thing."

Here you have another straightforward account of the first process of alchemy leading on to the beginning of the second. This is all the present author intends to present of the *Brief Guide*, for to give more at this juncture is but to lead to confusion. There is a good deal more, but its involved nature, much of which is padding, is best left alone until one is more advanced.

Perhaps it would help to recapitulate what has been said in the above work. Understand then that the alchemist takes four mercurial substances, namely four metals, as these are all alleged to have mercury as their base, and he reduces them to their two fundamental principles. In other words, we gather that most important secret that the end of the first process delivers into our hands two products made from the chaos or mixture of the four, and these are named sulphur and mercury. Take good notice now that really we have only one mass of matter, which may be easily divided into two, the sulphur and the mercury.

25

This sulphur and mercury are the elements with which all the books of the philosophers busy themselves. In the above *Brief Guide* it is revealed to the reader that here we have the "Rebis" or two things, so often mentioned, and we are also introduced to the two serpents constantly met with in the writings of the adepts. More than this, they are often referred to as "our gold and silver"; the latter is also termed "our mercury" because basically the sulphur is red in colour, and the mercury white; they are also called the red man and his white wife. Other names include Sun and Moon, king and queen, earth and water, male and female, and a few animals' names besides. Be ready therefore to recognise this pair whenever they are met with in alchemical literature.

To a great extent we have now cleared the ground of a good many blinds, stumbling blocks and misconceptions. This will bear fruit when we come to examine a complete treatise on the art of alchemy.

2. Sophic Fire

The time has come to provide a few hints for experiments and research work in the art of alchemy. The student is here warned not to undervalue the information that is being revealed, nor to imagine that the explanations now given are of little account. A wrong move may lead to anxious months of waiting for something which will never happen to take place. The farmer might just as well wait for crops that will never emerge from the ground. The prize is indeed fabulous, so the experimenter should not expect to find recipes as from a cookery book. This is not said facetiously, but purposely, because it has often been told that the whole art consists of first cooking, and later roasting; and this fact appears quite true.

To commence it is necessary to become acquainted with the following factors, each of which will be elucidated as we proceed.

(a) The principles or metals necessary to take in hand.
(b) The proportions of the ingredients which form the compounds.
(c) The kind of heating apparatus suitable for continuous use.
(d) The necessary vessels, their sizes and shapes.
(e) The correct temperatures to follow in the working.
(f) The periods of time during which to expect changes to take place.
(g) The colours and signs to be expected at each stage.

First it is advisable for the novice to try to gain some modern knowledge of metallurgy. With the aid of a simple textbook on the subject of metals, he can become acquainted with their characteristics (with which one has to work) and how they react to one another. One should know the colours they give off when wet and dry, their weight density and melting points, and how they agree or disagree when amalgamated with one another.

(a) The metals necessary to take in hand
Three are essential; and these are the salt, sulphur and mercury—or

the secret fire, sulphur and mercury. Gold or silver is the sulphur, mercury is prepared from antimony and iron, or a regulus of these two. The secret fire might be the name given to the mercury when prepared, or might be a kind of water which acts as a catalyst. These two names are always purposely mixed up, that is, one often being named for the other so that mistakes may be made, but in truth they are two different things. The secret fire which might be termed the fiery water dissolves the metals; this latter is a salt nitrate, often termed vinegar, to be found everywhere, easily, and never valued; yet never mentioned in any alchemical treatise by name. (A natural product found everywhere and in everything.)

(b) Proportions of the ingredients to form the first compound

From *The Marrow of Alchemy* by Philalethes: "Take of the red man one (iron); of the white wife three (antimony); and mix (which is a good proportion); then of the water four let there be . . . The mixture is our lead, which unto motion will be moved by a most gentle heat, which . . . This makes the regulus and will produce the mercury; and with the same proportion, add one part gold, which is the sulphur." Do not add the sulphur until the regulus is made.

(c) The type of heating apparatus for continuous use

A modern electrical hot-plate, with thermometer, and thermostat (one which must be reliable, for the fire must never go out from start to completion, through many months of watching). A hot-plate which will continue to function correctly when left for many days; and one on which the temperature may be raised as the processes are passed through. Heat used to start from 100°F. to 300°F. plus. The temperature is a great secret, as too cold may never achieve the desired objective, and too hot will spoil the work. Too hot drives all the liquid upward and the solid matter dries out for want of it.

(d) The vessels needed

Strong heat-resisting glass flasks with long necks, up to six inches. Glass retorts, scales, funnels, stone pestle and mortar and similar equipment used in modern chemistry. Sizes of flasks should be from 50 ml. to 250 ml. The closures to flasks must be airtight and perfect, else all will fail. Use modern rubber bungs or the glass may explode with the rarefying liquid, as the rubber bung is forced out instead of the flask exploding.

(e) *The correct temperatures*

Nature is simple in all her ways, and this art being a purely natural process, it is necessary that one holds in mind that everything that is carried out should be simple. In this art, nature brings about all the changes herself, after the conditions have been set, exactly as the farmer grows his produce. Digesting or cooking is all that nature needs, and not the heat of a furnace, at least not until the stone is made. A furnace is required later, but that should not be used except for the transmutation in which metals are melted in a crucible, with the Philosopher's Stone, and changed into gold or silver. Otherwise it is only dissolving and coagulating, "opening and shutting" as the alchemists term it, and this is best carried out on a hot-plate.

Fermentation, projection and transmutation occur after the red or white powder is produced, but as these will be dealt with later on in this book, for the time being we may leave them in abeyance.

(f) *The periods before changes can be expected*

These are doubtful, depending upon the correct heat, the proportions used, and other factors, but most adepts say forty-two days to the black stage, ninety days to the white stage, and five months to the red stage which signifies completion. Once the powder is made these times may be reduced to a few days to make any amount more with the finished product.

(g) *The colours and signs to be expected*

Sir George Ripley, Canon of Bridlington, who flourished in the days of Edward IV, wrote some books on the art, of which the chief one, a lengthy poem, was entitled *The Twelve Gates of Alchemy*. This poem was divided into twelve parts, and each part was presented as a gate. The titles of the gates taken altogether, give the whole secret and details of the working, from the beginning to completion. Note however that nowhere is there given the names of any actual metals to be used in the art of alchemy! Later these *Twelve Gates* will be fully presented in Chapter 8 of this book, but for the present their titles are useful, in that they outline the sequence of alchemical operations.

1. Calcination	Reducing the principles to atoms, but not by burning.
2. Dissolution	Dissolving the metals, time and nature doing the work.
3. Separation	Separating the light parts from the heavy parts.
4. Conjunction	Joining the principles. Amalgamating the elements.
5. Putrefaction	The first change to be seen. Blackness appearing.
6. Congealation	The liquidised matter congeals, or solidifies.
7. Cibation	When the matter in the vessels appear dry, it is wetted again.
8. Sublimation	Extraction by volatilisation or distillation.
9. Fermentation	Adding the required precious metal as a yeast to empower the powder or stone to transmute.
10. Exaltation	Raising the power or virtue enabling it to transmute.
11. Multiplation	Raising the quantity and quality of the powder or stone.
12. Projection	The work of transmutation into gold and silver.

If these twelve processes appear formidable to the beginner, remember the alchemists' saying, that it is "child's play and woman's work"! Much of the work is done by nature; we are also told that "there must be no laying on of hands", or moving the vessel, once the conditions are set. By analogy, the farmer's work could easily be divided into twelve divisions in the same way. Preparing the land and sowing the seed could be represented by several of the gates; what follows and is carried out by nature, could be categorised under a few more, until the results are ready for gathering; then the farmer's work in harvesting might be represented by the remaining gates. This is one example of the working of the twelve gates and could represent the working and meaning of the three processes that have been mentioned earlier in this book.

Next, in order to mislead the student, some cunning adepts have denied that metals are the basic matter of the Philosophers' Stone. There must be no doubt at all on this point, for to make gold and silver from any other matter is absolutely senseless. This piece of guile has wasted the lives of many searchers.

Another difficulty has been the claim of some treatises that "one only thing" is the matter of the stone, while others claim any number up to seven. The reader is advised to ignore these quibbles. Indeed when the stone is made, it all comes to one thing, and only three metals are used. The rest only come into use at transmutation into gold or silver, after the red or white powder is made.

Finally, it is of the utmost importance to remember there are three stages or processes to pass through before the completion of the Philosophers' Stone. The reader might ask why this is so important. Well, the answer is that processes are mentioned at various times, but rarely whether they are the first, second or third; and this must be specially noted, that the first or starting point is hardly ever mentioned, for this beginning is the greatest secret of all, and it is hidden, suppressed and ignored by all the philosophers. If a hint is ever dropped, it is never indicated which matter they are talking about. In fact, so well has this been done that the beginner could be entirely oblivious of it. Yet note well, whole treatises have been written about this first hidden matter, which is nothing else but the preparation known as the "Secret Fire" which is not a metal at all, but the very necessary catalyst for melting all the metals. The "Secret Fire" is also the prepared mercury.

To sum up, to make the Philosophers' Stone, three items are used, but never vulgar mercury or quicksilver. Then there is a water or "secret fire" which is the catalyst and which some adepts have called mercury.

Even when it is guessed that metals were the basic components (many treatises never speak of anything at all to work on) one is still not given some method of beginning experiments. The small number of scientists who wrote books on the subject of alchemy in the last fifty years certainly did not know. The adepts, in their books, always speak of salt, sulphur and mercury, which principles in use are *none* of the three we know under those names. In the various stages of alchemy, the metals have so changed their appearance, colours and texture, becoming a slime, powder or soot, that they can hardly be called metals at all, and the artful masters of the art have taken full advantage of this to mislead and mystify the tyro. When some wrote that metals are not used in alchemy, they felt that evasive information of this kind was speaking the truth, but this half-truth was a downright lie to the student, who knew that an apple is still an apple even when changed into a pie.

31

Most of the old writers on alchemy have treated the subject of the art as though it was one continuous process from beginning to the end, but as already said, it is performed in three stages; each when finished is preparatory to the next. However, very rarely did they put these in the correct order, the first stage was almost always ignored, and they mostly started at the last!

A quotation which confirms this is taken from a book entitled *Ripley Revived,* a commentary on Ripley by Philalethes who lived in the seventeenth century:

"And in the first place, we shall treat of the regimen of mercury, which is a secret hitherto not discovered by any philosophers; for they verily do begin their work at the second regimen, and so give the young practitioner no light in the magistery in the capital signs of blackness; on this point that good Marquis of Trevisan was silent . . . and therefore he passeth over in silence the first and most intricate regimen which is forty or fifty days ere it is fully complete, in which time the poor practitioner is left to uncertain experiments and so remains a great space, and this secret before me no man has ever yet found discovered."

The blackness spoken of here is the result of the work of the first stage, in which the metals turn into a black slime. This indeed is the key spoken of which opens the door to all the rest of the work, for knowing this, one has the general idea of how to do the whole work, because the truth is that all the stages follow the same routine.

A great deal more might be added to round out the picture of alchemy for those newly come to the science, but it would be better to proceed by examining the first book, and then go on to explain, by adding extracts here and there to bear out what is being elucidated.

The first book chosen is entitled *The Sophic Fire* by John Pontanus, a master of alchemy who lived in the Middle Ages. This particular book is taken from among a great number, because it is succinct, direct to the heart of the subject, and without evasion and prevarication. More than this, this treatise truthfully points out to the searcher a book that stands out like a welcome beacon to point the way to success in the art. We will speak of this book later. Meanwhile here is the *Sophic Fire* in full. Brackets indicate comments by the present author.

THE SOPHIC FIRE
by John Pontanus

"I, John Pontanus, have travelled through many countries, that I might know the certainty of the philosophers' stone: and I found many deceivers, but no true philosophers, which put me upon incessant studying, and making many doubts, till at length I found out the truth. But when I had attained the knowledge of the matter in general, yet I erred at least two hundred times, before I could attain to know the singular thing itself, with the work and practice thereof.

"First, I began with the putrefaction of the matter, which I continued for nine months together, and obtained nothing. I then for some certain time tried a 'Balneum Marie' [a warm water bath], but in vain. After that, I used a fire of calcination for three months space, and still found myself out of the way. I essayed all sorts of distillations and sublimations, as the philosophers, Geber, Archelaus, and all the rest of them have prescribed, and yet found nothing: In sum, I attempted to perfect the whole work of alchemy by all imaginable and likely means—as by horse-dung [this is a specification of a heat used], baths, ashes, and other heats of divers kinds, all which are found in philosophers' books, yet without success. I yet continually for three years together studied the books of the philosophers, and that chiefly in Hermes [he is known as the father of alchemy], whose concise words comprehend the sum of the whole matter [maybe, but hopeless to follow until one knows the work], viz. the secret of the philosophers' stone, by an obscure way of speaking, of what is superior, and what is inferior, to wit, of heaven and earth. Therefore our operation which brings the matter into being, in the first, second, and third work [take good notice of three stages, which processes are rarely mentioned anywhere], is not any of those things mentioned above and found in the books of the philosophers. Shall I demand then, what it is that perfects the work, since the wise men have thus concealed it? Truly, being moved with a generous spirit, I will declare it, with the complement of the whole work.

"The Lapis Philosophorum, therefore, is but one, though it has many names, which before you conceive them, will be very difficult. For it is watery [liquid], airy [volatile], fiery, earthy: it is salt, sulphur, mercury, and phlegm; it is sulphureous, yet is argent vive [twice here, quicksilver is mentioned]; it has many superfluities, which are turned into the true essence by the help of our fire. ['Our fire' is not just ordinary fire and notice that the subject mentioned here is 'fiery'. Could this be our fire? This 'our fire' is the greatest secret of alchemy, and usually known in the art as the 'Secret Fire'.] He that separates anything from the subject or matter, thinking it to be necessary, wholly errs in his philosophy. [This is said because most adepts write that one must separate the clean from the muddy or dirty matter, but one must know what is clean and what is dirty. In the first stage everything is changed into wet mud, or dry soot, even gold and silver look like this.] That which is superfluous, unclean, filthy, feculent, and in a word, the whole substance of the subject is transmuted or changed in a perfect, fixed, and spiritual body, by the help of our fire, which the wise men never revealed, and therefore it is, that few attain to this art, as thinking that to be superfluous and impure, which is not. [In alchemy, a fixed metal is one that remains the same no matter what is done with it, or however treated. Now Pontanus proceeds to speak of the character of 'our Fire', which is not fire but acts, in fact, more powerfully than any fire.]

"It behoves us now to enquire after the properties of 'our fire', and how it agrees with our matter, according to that which I have said, viz. that a transmutation may be made, though the fire is not such as to burn the matter, separating nothing from it, nor dividing the pure parts from the impure, as the philosophers teach [now you can understand why it is hopeless to study most of the alchemical treatises, for most of them are written to mislead, unless you already know the stumbling blocks], but our fire transmutes and changes the whole subject into purity. Nor does it sublime after the manner of Geber's sublimation, nor the sublimations or distillations of Arnoldous, or others: but it is perfected in a short time. [Pontanus continues to say how misleading most adepts are in their works, and goes on to explain the characteristics of 'our fire'.]

"It is a matter mineral, equal, continuous, vapours or fumes not, unless too much provoked; partakes of sulphur, and is taken otherwise than from matter. It destroys all things, dissolves, congeals, coagulates and calcines, adapted to penetrate, and is a compendium, without any great cost. And that is the fire, with a gentle heat, soft or remiss, by which the whole work is perfected, with all the proper sublimations. [Take good notice of what follows, and go no further than this book, else you are lost in a maze of instructions which will utterly confuse.] They who read Geber, with all the rest of the philosophers, though they should survive a hundred thousand years, yet they would not be able to comprehend it, for that this fire is found by a profound cogitation only, which being once apprehended, may then be gathered out of books—and not before.

"The error, therefore, in this work, proceeds chiefly from a not knowing or understanding of the true fire, which is one of the moving principles that transmutes the whole matter into the true philosophers' stone; and therefore diligently find it out. Had I found that first, I had never been two hundred times mistaken in the pursuit of the matter I so long sought after. For which cause sake, I wonder not that so many, and so great men, have not attained unto the work. They have erred, they do err, and they will err; because the philosophers, *Artephius only excepted*, have concealed the principle or proper agent. And unless I had read Artephius, and sensibly understood his speech, I had never arrived to the complement of the work.

"Now the principal part is this: Let the matter be taken and diligently ground with a philosophical contrition, put upon the fire, with such a proportion of heat that it only excite or stir up the matter; and in short time that fire, without any laying on of hands, will complete the whole work, because it putrefies, corrupts, generates and perfects the whole work, and makes the three principal colours, viz. the black, white and red to appear. And by the means of this our fire, the medicine will be multiplied by the addition of the crude matter, not only in quantity, but also in quality or virtue. Therefore seek out this fire with all thy industry, for having once found it, thou shalt accomplish thy desire, because it performs the whole work, and is the true key of all the philisophers, which they never yet revealed. Consider well of what I have spoken, otherwise it will be hid from thine eyes.

"Being moved with generosity, I have written these things, that I might speak plainly, this fire is not transmuted with the matter, because it is nothing of the matter, as I have before declared and these things I have thought fit to speak, as a warning to the prudent

35

sons of art, that they spend not their money unprofitably, but may know what they ought to look after; for by this only they may attain to the perfection of the secret, and by no other means."

The above short treatise speaks of one matter only, and is presumably the most important key to the whole art. For this "Sophic Fire", or "our fire", is the great secret without which nothing can be achieved. This Secret Fire, by which it is now known, is not a fire at all, is vital, and acts as a catalyst; it moves the matter onwards to its completion from beginning to end, but always with the aid of an exterior heat which must be gentle; "the heat of a summer's day, or a chicken on her eggs". In fact, so powerful is this Secret Fire that one is advised to leave the work to nature, without the "laying on of hands".

Note that Pontanus calls this Secret Fire "Argent Vivé", and mercury, among other things. Now ordinary mercury is "the villain of the piece" in every book ever written on the art, and if ever crude mercury is mentioned at all, it is always with the warning that the searcher can expect only failure if this metal is used.

Once again, remember the old writers were always on their guard lest they should inadvertently divulge any information of too much significance. Nevertheless, true bits of knowledge are strewn about everywhere, and it behoves the searcher to pick them up. Therefore what follows are curious extracts which have been taken from many important books, which tell the researcher in the plainest manner all that he needs to know. In fact what the "secret fire" is; what mercury is (or rather what the alchemist calls his mercury), in short the universal solvent of all metals.

Now to the first extract—from the *Epistles of Ali-Puli*, entitled the *Concentrated Centre of Nature*:

"I say to you, my students in the study of nature, if you do not find the thing for which you are seeking, in your own self, much less will you find it outside yourself. Understand the glorious strength resident in your own selves. Why trouble to enquire from another? In man named after God, there are things more glorious than to be found anywhere else in the world. Should anyone desire to become a master, he will not find a better material for his achievement anywhere than in himself. Oh, man know thyself. In you resides the treasure of all treasures. Unknowingly this is the great wonder of the world. It is in reality a burning water, a liquid fire, more potent than all fire. In its crude state, it dissolves and absorbs solid gold. It reduces it into a fatty black grey earth, and a thick slimy salt water, without fire or acid, and without any violent reaction, which no other thing in the world can accomplish. Nothing is excluded from it, and though it is the most costly thing in the world, a king cannot possess more of it than a beggar, the wise men of old sought for it and found it.

"Seek for it, my friends, in every way and in everything, though maybe you do not know the hidden source of its origin; and even if you should come to find it, yet you would not have any idea of the aspect of things to be seen within it. Yet I will be explicit; it is a spiritual water, a true spirit, the spirit of life itself. Surely I may be justified in proclaiming: O, water, magnificent, illuminating, sweet; O, bitter and obscure, which strengthens us until the day of our death. This is the foundation stone in truth, which is rejected by the careless ignorance of the builders, and the alchemists even to this day."

Another curious piece of writing, medieval style, from *Experience & Philosophy*, a treatise included in *Theatrum Chemicum* published in 1613, also speaks of the wonderful and mysterious water. In a way it is rather amusing to see how these alchemists were bursting to tell someone of their discoveries, yet buried them more deeply, ever terribly afraid to speak out plainly: making a gesture of giving, before quickly grabbing back their revelation.

> "One thing was first employed,
> And shall not be destroyed,
> It compasseth the world around,
> A matter easy to be found:
> And yet most hardest to come by,
> A secret of secrets, pardye,
> That is most vile and least set by,
> And it is my love and darling,
> Conceived with all living things,
> And travels to the worlds ending."

There are no less than sixteen of these poetic sets, but as one is not likely to learn much from them, this one will be enough.

The following extract will present the reader with a typical example of a misleading text. Eirenæus Philalethes, an adept who wrote many books, repeatedly assured us "that never was the art so plainly discovered", but alas he also confesses to deception:

"Such passages as these, we do sometimes use when we speak of the preparation of our mercury, and this we do to deceive the simple, and it is also for no other end that we confound our operations, speaking of one when we ought to speak of another. For if this art were plainly set down, our operations would be contemptible even to the foolish. Therefore believe me in this, that because our works are truly natural, we therefore take the liberty to confound the philosopher's work with that which is purely nature's work, so that we might keep the simple in ignorance concerning our true vinegre, which being unknown, their labour is wholly lost."

The above extract confirms what has so far been said concerning misleading texts, but in addition there are some interesting hints in it. Notice first the hint that "their mercury" has to be prepared; in this manner informing us that this preparation of "our mercury" is a first step and a process on its own. In the last sentence, Philalethes calls the mercury vinegre, the nature of which is bitter, biting, sharp. One more hint here, and that is that there is more than one process in the work. Yet other adepts have asserted that there is but one continuous process from beginning to the end.

Alchemical literature is saturated with this kind of poetry, full of riddles, parables, allegories, metaphors, and all sorts of claptrap, which may be ignored when met with, otherwise all kinds of crazy notions will take root in the mind to the detriment of your research.

And now perhaps it will be better to entertain something more modern and simple. This comes from the *Hermetic Triumph* published in 1723. There are two treatises in this book and this one is entitled *The Six Keys of Eudoxus*. Keep in mind we are still only dealing with the fiery water which is the universal solvent, the sophic mercury, and not common mercury.

'The first key is that which opens the dark prisons, in which the

sulphur is shut up; this is it which knows how to extract the seed out of the body, which forms the stone of the philosophers by the conjunction of the male and the female; of the spirit with the body; of sulphur with mercury. Hermes has manifestly demonstrated the operation of this first key by these words; In the caverns of the metals; there is hidden the stone which is venerable, bright in colour, a mind sublime and an open sea. This stone has a bright glittering; it contains a spirit of a sublime original; it is the sea of the wise, in which they fish for their mysterious fish."
(The open sea, and the sea of the wise is the fiery water.)

Studying alchemical writings, the student will repeatedly come across the claim that alchemy is carried out with "one only thing", and because all the metals are mentioned, as used in the working in different books, the experimenter is forever perplexed wondering what can be meant by this, since obviously so many different things are named. Finally, one comes to the conclusion that this is another misleading lie. But it need not be a lie at all, for "one only thing" refers to the water without which nothing can be achieved, and this water is indeed the supreme secret, and until this is discovered, and its manner of preparation, all is a waste of time.

One more extract about the *Sophic Fire*:

"What is the Alkahest? It is a Universal Menstruum, and in a word may be called, Ignis-Aqua, a fiery water, an uncompounded and immortal ens, which is penetrative, resolving all things into their first liquid matter; nor can anything resist its power, for it acts without any reaction from the patient, nor does it suffer anything but its equal, by which it is brought into subjection; but after it has dissolved all things, it remaineth entire in its former nature, and is of the same virtue after a thousand operations as at the first."

3. The Secret Book

In the alchemical art, the seven metals usually mentioned are named after the planets. For example, copper is known as Venus, and where referred to, the student is advised that he should treat it as a symbol of love, or as a conductor, rather than a metal, for as a metal it is of little use in the art of alchemy. Lead is called Saturn, and indicates something dark, black, or forbidding in appearance. Tin, copper and lead are problem metals; tin is connected with the making of silvery compounds, and copper, although it acts as a conductor in the compound of metals, is usually considered of little use in the alchemic process.

However, there is an eighth metal, rarely met with in the many treatises, and then it is usually passed over as though of no account. Yet it is of the greatest importance, for without it nothing may be achieved. Fortunate indeed is the researcher who notices it: the metal is *antimony*.

We will see in the *Secret Book* of Artephius, which John Pontanus found to be the only book among thousands which could be relied on, and which he recommended above all others, that the first word is antimony. Note, however, that the order of the text is not sequential.

THE SECRET BOOK
by Artephius (twelfth century)

1. Antimony is a mineral participating of saturnine parts, and has in all respects the nature thereof. This saturnine antimony agrees with sol, and contains in itself argent vive, in which no metal is

swallowed up, except gold; and gold is truly swallowed up by this antimonial argent vive. Without this argent vive no metal whatsoever can be whitened; it whitens laton, i.e. gold; reduceth a perfect body into its prima materia, or first matter, viz. into sulphur and argent vive, of a white colour, and outshining a looking glass. It dissolves, I say the perfect body, which is so in its own nature; for this water is friendly and agreeable with the metals, whitening sol, because it contains in itself white or pure argent vive.

2. And from both these you may draw a great arcanum, viz. a water of saturnine antimony, mercurial and white; to the end that it may whiten sol, not burning, but dissolving, and afterwards congealing to the consistence or likeness of white cream. Therefore, saith the philosopher, this water makes the body to be volatile; because after it has been dissolved in it, and infrigidated, it ascends above and swims upon the surface of the water. Take, saith he, crude leaf gold, or calcined with mercury, and put it into our vinegre, made of saturnine antimony, mercurial, and sal ammoniac, in a broad glass vessel, and four inches high or more; put it into a gentle heat, and in a short time you will see elevated a liquor, as it were oil swimming atop, much like a scum. Gather this with a spoon or a feather dipping it in; and in so doing often times a day until nothing more arises; evaporate the water with a gentle heat, i.e., the superfluous humidity of the vinegre, and there will remain the quintessence, potestates or powers of gold in the form of a white oil incombustible. In this oil the philosophers have placed their greatest secrets; it is exceeding sweet, and of great virtue for easing the pains of wounds

3. The whole, then, of this antimonial secret is, that we know how by it to extract or draw forth argent vive, out of the body of Magnesia, not burning, and this is antimony, and a mercurial sublimate. That is, you must extract a living and incombustible water, and then congeal, or coagulate it with the perfect body of sol, i.e. fine gold, without alloy; which is done by dissolving it into a nature and white substance of the consistency of cream, and made thoroughly white. But first this sol by putrefaction and resolution in this water, loseth all its light and brightness, and will grow dark and black; afterwards it will ascend above the water, and by little and little will swim upon it, in a substance of a white colour. And this is the whitening of red laton to sublimate it philosophically, and to reduce

it into its first matter; viz. into a white incombustible sulphur, and into a fixed argent vive. Thus the perfect body of sol, resumeth life in this water; it is revived, inspired, grows, and is multiplied in its kind, as all other things are. For in this water, it so happens, that the body compounded of two bodies, viz. sol and luna, is puffed up, swells, putrefies, is raised up, and does increase by the receiving from the vegetable and animated nature and substance.

4. Our water also, or vinegar aforesaid, is the vinegar of the mountains, i.e. of sol and luna; and therefore it is mixed with gold and silver, and sticks close to them perpetually; and the body receiveth from this water a white tincture, and shines with inestimable brightness. Who so therefore knows how to convert, or change the body into a medicinal white gold, may easily by the same white gold change all imperfect metals into the best and finest silver. And this white gold is called by the philosophers "luna alba philosophorum, argentum vivum album fixum, aurum alchymiae, and fumus albus": and therefore without this our antimonial vinegar, the aurum album of the philosophers cannot be made. And because in our vinegar there is a double substance of argentum vivum, the one from antimony, and the other from mercury sublimated, it does give a double weight and substance of fixed argent vive, and also augments therein the native colour, weight, substance, and tincture thereof.

5. Our dissolving water therefore carries with it a great tincture, and a great melting or dissolving; because that when it feels the vulgar fire, if there be in it the pure and fine bodies of sol or luna, it immediately melts them, and converts them into its white substance such as itself is, and gives to the body colour, weight, and tincture. In it also is a powder of liquefying or melting all things that can be melted or dissolved; it is a water ponderous, viscous, precious, and worthy to be esteemed, resolving all crude bodies into their prima materia, or first matter, viz. earth and a viscous powder; that is into sulphur, and argentum vivum. If therefore you put into this water, leaves, filings, or calx of any metal, and set it in a gentle heat for a time, the whole will be dissolved, and converted into a viscous water, or white oil, as aforesaid. Thus it mollifies the body, and prepares for liquefaction; yea, it makes all things fusible, viz. stones and metals, and after gives them spirit and life. And it dissolves all things with an admirable solution, transmuting the perfect body into a

fusible medicine, melting, or liquefying, moreover fixing, and augmenting the weight and colour.

6. Work therefore with it, and you shall obtain from it what you desire, for it is the spirit and soul of sol and luna; it is the oil, the dissolving water, the fountain, the Balneum Mariae, the praeternatural fire, the moist fire, the secret, hidden and invisible fire. It is also the most acrid vinegar, concerning which an ancient philosopher saith, I besought the Lord, and he showed me a pure clear water, which I knew to be the pure vinegar, altering, penetrating, and digesting. I say a penetrating vinegar, and the moving instrument for putrefying, resolving and reducing gold or silver into their prima materia or first matter. And it is the only agent in the universe, which in this art is able to reincrudate metallic bodies with the conservation of their species. It is therefore the only apt and natural medium, by which we ought to resolve the perfect bodies of sol and luna, by a wonderful and solemn dissolution, with the conservation of the species, and without any distruction, unless it be to a new, more noble, and better form or generation, viz. into the perfect philosophers' stone, which is their wonderful secret and arcanum.

7. Now this water is a certain middle substance, clear as fine silver, which ought to receive the tinctures of sol and luna, so as they may be congealed, and changed into a white and living earth. For this water needs the perfect bodies, that with them after the dissolution, it may be congealed, fixed, and coagulated into a white earth. But if this solution is also their coagulation, for they have one and the same operation, because one is not dissolved, but the other is congealed, nor is there any other water which can dissolve the bodies, but that which abideth with them in the matter and the form. It cannot be permanent unless it be of the nature of other bodies, that they may be made one. When therefore you see the water coagulate itself with the bodies that be dissolved therein; be assured that thy knowledge, way of working, and the work itself are true and philosophic, and that you have done rightly according to art.

8. Thus you see that nature has to be amended by its own like nature; that is, gold and silver are to be exalted in our water, as our water also with these bodies; which water is called the medium of the soul, without which nothing has to be done in this art. It is a vegetable, mineral, and animal fire, which conserves the fixed spirits of sol and luna, but destroys and conquers their bodies; for it

44

destroys, overturns, and changes bodies and metallic forms, making them to be no bodies but a fixed spirit. And it turns them into a humid substance, soft and fluid, which hath ingression and power to enter into other imperfect bodies, and to mix with them in their smallest parts, and to tinge and make them perfect. But this they could not do while they remained in their metallic forms or bodies, which were dry and hard, whereby they could have no entrance into other things, so to tinge and make perfect, what was before imperfect.

9. It is necessary therefore to convert the bodies of metals into a fluid substance; for that every tincture will tinge a thousand times more in a soft and liquid substance, than when it is in a dry one, as is plainly apparent in saffron. Therefore the transmutation of imperfect metals, is impossible to be done by perfect bodies, while they are dry and hard; for which cause sake they must be brought back into their first matter, which is soft and fluid. It appears therefore that the moisture must be reverted that the hidden treasure may be revealed. And this is called the reincrudation of bodies, which is the decocting and softening them, till they lose their hard and dry substance or form; because that which is dry doth not enter into, nor tinge anything except its own body, nor can it be tinged except it be tinged; because, as I said before, a thick dry earthy matter does not penetrate nor tinge, and therefore, because it cannot enter or penetrate, it can make no alteration in the matter to be altered. For this reason it is, that gold coloureth not, until its internal or hidden spirit is drawn forth out of its bowels by this, our white water, and that it may be made altogether a spiritual substance, a white vapour, a white spirit, and a wonderful soul.

10. It behoves us therefore by this our water to attenuate, alter and soften the perfect bodies, to wit sol and luna, that so they may be mixed other imperfect bodies. From whence, if we had no other benefit by this our antimonial water, than that it rendered bodies soft, more subtile, and fluid, according to its own nature, it would be sufficient. But more than that, it brings back bodies to their original of sulphur and mercury, that of them we may afterwards in a little time, in less than an hour's time do that above ground which nature was a thousand years doing underground, in the mines of the earth, which is a work almost miraculous.

11. And therefore our ultimate, or highest secret is, by this our

45

water, to make bodies volatile, spiritual, and a tincture, or tinging water, which may have ingress or entrance into bodies; for it makes bodies to be merely spirit, because it reduces hard and dry bodies, and prepares them for fusion, melting, or dissolving; that is, it converts them into a permanent or fixed water. And so it makes of bodies a most precious and desirable oil, which is the true tincture, and the permanent fixed white water, by nature hot and moist, or rather temperate, subtile, fusible as wax, which does penetrate, sink, tinge, and make perfect the work. And this our water immediately dissolves bodies (as sol and luna) and makes them into an incombustible oil, which then may be mixed with other imperfect bodies. It also converts other bodies into the nature of a fusible salt which the philosophers call "sal alebrot philosophorum", better and more noble than any other salt, being in its own nature fixed and not subject to vanish in fire. It is an oil indeed by nature hot, subtile, penetrating, sinking through and entering into other bodies; it is called the perfect or great elixir, and the hidden secret of the wise searchers of nature. He therefore that knows this salt of sol and luna, and its generation and preparation, and afterwards how to commix it, and make it homogene with other imperfect bodies, he in truth knows one of the greatest secrets of nature, and the only way that leads to perfection.

12. These bodies thus dissolved by our water are called argent vive, which is not without its sulphur, nor sulphur without the fixedness of sol and luna; because sol and luna are the particular means, or medium in the form through which nature passes in the perfecting or the completing thereof. And this argent vive is called our esteemed and valuable salt, being animated and pregnant, and our fire, for that is nothing but fire; yet not fire, but sulphur; and not sulphur only, but also quicksilver drawn from sol and luna by our water, and reduced to a stone of great price. That is to say it is a matter or substance of sol and luna, or silver and gold, altered from vileness to nobility. Now you must note that this white sulphur is the father and mother of the metals; it is our mercury, and the mineral of gold; also the soul, and the ferment; yea, the mineral virtue, and the living body; our sulphur, and our quicksilver; that is, sulphur of sulphur, quicksilver of quicksilver, and mercury of mercury.

13. The property therefore of our water is, that it melts or dissolves gold and silver, and increases their native tincture or colour.

46

For it changes their bodies from being corporeal, into a spirituality; and it is in this water which turns the bodies, or corporeal substance into a white vapour, which is a soul which is whiteness itself, subtile, hot and full of fire. This water also called the tinging or blood-colour-making stone, being the virtue of the spiritual tincture, without which nothing can be done; and is the subject of all things that can be melted, and of liquefaction itself, which agrees perfectly and unites closely with sol and luna from which it can never be separated. For it joined in affinity to the gold and silver, but more immediately to the gold than to the silver; which you are to take special notice of. It is also called the medium of conjoining the tinctures of sol and luna with the inferior or imperfect metals; for it turns the bodies into the true tincture, to tinge the said other imperfect metals, also it is the water that whiteneth, as it is whiteness itself, which quickeneth, as it is a soul; and therefore as the philosopher saith, quickly entereth into its body.

14. For it is a living water which comes to moisten the earth, that it may spring out, and in its due season bring forth much fruit; for all things springing from the earth, are endued through dew and moisture. The earth therefore springeth not forth without watering and moisture; it is the water proceeding from May dew that cleanseth the body; and like rain it penetrates them, and makes one body of two bodies. This aqua vitae or water of life, being rightly ordered and disposed with the body, it whitens it, and converts or changes it into its white colour, for this water is a white vapour, and therefore the body is whitened with it. It behoves you therefore to whiten the body, and open its unfoldings, for between these two, that is between the body and the water, there is desire and friendship, like as between male and female, because of the propinquity and likeness of their natures.

15. Now this our second and living water is called "Azoth", the water washing the laton, viz. the body compounded of sol and luna by our first water; it is also called the soul of the dissolved bodies, which souls we have even now tied together, for the use of the wise philosopher. How precious then, and how great a thing is this water; for without it, the work could never be done or perfected; it is also called the "vase naturae", the belly, the womb, the receptacle of the tincture, the earth, the nurse. It is the royal fountain in which the king and queen bathe themselves; and the mother must be put into

and sealed up within the belly of her infant; and that is sol himself, who proceeded from her, and whom she brought forth; and therefore they have loved one another as mother and son, and are conjoined together, because they come from one and the same root, and are of the same substance and nature. And because this water is the water of the vegetable life, it causes the dead body to vegetate, increase and spring forth, and to rise from death to life, by being dissolved first and then sublimed. And in doing this the body is converted into a spirit, and the spirit afterwards into a body; and then is made the amity, the peace, the concord, and the union of the contraries, to wit, between the body and the spirit, which reciprocally, or mutually change their natures which they receive, and communicate one to another through their most minute parts, so that that which is hot is mixed with that which is cold, the dry with the moist, and the hard with the soft; by which means, there is a mixture made of contrary natures, viz. of cold with hot, and moist with dry, even a most admirable unity between enemies.

16. Our dissolution then of bodies, which is made such in this first water, is nothing else, but a destroying or overcoming of the moist with the dry, for the moist is coagulated with the dry. For the moisture is contained under, terminated with, and coagulated in the dry body, to wit, in that which is earthy. Let therefore the hard and the dry bodies be put into our first water in a vessel, which close well, and there let them abide till they be dissolved, and ascend to the top; then may they be called a new body, the white gold made by art, the white stone, the white sulphur, not inflammable, the paradisical stone, viz. the stone transmuting imperfect metals into white silver. Then have we also the body, soul, and spirit altogether; of which the spirit and soul it is said, that they cannot be extracted from the perfect bodies, but by the help or conjunction of our dissolving water. Because it is certain, that the things fixed cannot be lifted up, or made to ascend, but by the conjunction or help of that which is volatile.

17. The spirit, therefore, by help of the water and the soul, is drawn forth from the bodies themselves, and the body is thereby made spiritual; for that at the same instant of time, the spirit, with the soul of the bodies, ascends on high to the superior part, which is the perfection of the stone and is called sublimation. This sublimation, is made by things acid, spiritual, volatile, and which are in their

own nature sulphureous and viscous, which dissolves bodies and makes them to ascend, and be changed into air and spirit. And in this sublimation, a certain part of our said first water ascends with the bodies, joining itself with them, ascending and subliming into one neutral and complex substance, which contains the nature of the two, viz. the nature of the two bodies and the water. And therefore it is called the corporeal and spiritual compositum, corjufle, cambar, ethelia, zandarith, duenech, the good; but properly it is called the permanent or fixed water only, because it flies not in the fire. But it perpetually adheres to the commixed or compound bodies, that is, the sol and luna, and communicates to them the living tincture, incombustible and most fixed, much more noble and precious than the former which those bodies had. Because from henceforth this tincture runs like oil, running through and penetrating bodies, and giving to them its wonderful fixity; and this tincture is the spirit, and the spirit is the soul, and the soul is the body. For in this operation, the body is made a spirit of a most subtile nature; and again, the spirit is corporified and changed into the nature of the body, with the bodies, whereby our stone consists of a body, a soul, and a spirit.

18. O God, how through nature, doth thou change a body into a spirit: which could not be done, if the spirit were not incorporated with the bodies, and the bodies made volatile with the spirit, and afterwards permanent and fixed. For this cause sake, they have passed over into one another, and by the influence of wisdom, are converted the one into the other. O Wisdom: how thou makest the most fixed gold to be volatile and fugitive, yea, though by nature it is the most fixed of all things in the world. It is necessary therefore, to dissolve and liquefy these bodies by our water, and to make them a permanent or fixed water, a pure, golden water leaving in the bottom the gross, earthy, superfluous and dry matter. And in this subliming, making thin and pure, the fire ought to be gentle; but if in this subliming with a soft fire, the bodies be not purified, and the gross and the earthy parts thereof (note this well) be not separated from the impurities of the dead, you shall not be able to perfect the work. For thou needest nothing but the thin and subtile part of the dissolved bodies, which our water will give thee, if thou proceedest with a slow or gentle fire, by separating the things heterogene from the things homogene.

19. This compositum then has its mundification or cleaning, by

our moist fire, which by dissolving and subliming that which is pure and white, it cast forth its faeces or filth like a voluntary vomit, for in such a dissolution and natural sublimation or lifting up, there is a loosening or untying of the elements, and a cleansing and separating of the pure from the impure. So that the pure and white substance ascends upwards and the impure and earthy remains fixed in the bottom of the water and the vessel. This must be taken away and removed, because it is of no value, taking only the middle white substance, flowing and melted or dissolved, rejecting the feculent earth, which remains below in the bottom. These faeces were separated partly by the water, and are the dross and terra damnata, which is of no value, nor can do any such service as the clear, white, pure and clear matter, which is wholly and only to be taken and made use of.

20. And against this capharean rock, the ship of knowledge, or art of the young philosopher is often, as it happened also to me sometimes, dashed together in pieces, or destroyed, because the philosophers for the most part speak by the contraries. That is to say that nothing must be removed or taken away, except the moisture, which is the blackness; which notwithstanding they speak and write only to the unwary, who, without a master, indefatigable reading, or humble supplications to God Almighty, would ravish away the golden fleece. It is therefore to be observed, that this separation, division, and sublimation, is without doubt the key to the whole work.

4. The Wisdom of Artephius

21. After the putrefaction, then and dissolution of these bodies, our bodies also ascend to the top, even to the surface of the dissolving water, in a whiteness of colour, which whiteness is life. And in this whiteness, the antimonial and mercurial soul, is by natural compact infused into, and joined with the spirits of sol and luna, which separate the thin from the thick, and the pure from the impure. That is, by lifting up, by little and little, the thin and the pure part of the body, from the faeces and impurity, until all the pure parts are separated and ascended. And in this work is our natural and philosophical sublimation work completed. Now in this whiteness is the soul infused into the body, to wit, the mineral virtue, which is more subtile than fire, being indeed the true quintessence and life, which desires or hungers to be born again, and to put off the defilements and be spoiled of its gross and earthy faeces, which it has taken from its monstrous womb, and corrupt place of its original. And in this our philosophical sublimation, not in the impure, corrupt, vulgar mercury, which has no qualities or properties like to those, with which our mercury, drawn from its vitriolic caverns is adorned. But let us return to our sublimation.

22. It is most certain therefore in this art, that this soul extracted from the bodies, cannot be made to ascend, but by adding to it a volatile matter, which is of its own kind. By which the bodies will be made volatile and spiritual, lifting themselves up, subtilizing and subliming themselves, contrary to their own proper nature, which is corporeal, heavy, and ponderous. And by this means they are unbodied, or made no bodies, to wit, incorporeal, and a quintessence of the nature of a spirit, which is called, "avis hermetis", and "mercurius extractus", drawn from a red subject or matter. And so the terrene or earthy parts remain below, or rather the grosser parts of the bodies, which can by no industry or ingenuity of man be brought to a perfect dissolution.

23. And this white vapour, this white gold, to wit, this quintes-

sence, is called also the compound magnesia, which like a man does contain, or like man is composed of a body, soul and spirit. Now the body is the fixed solar earth, exceeding the most subtile matter, which by the help of our divine water is with difficulty lifted up or separated. The soul is the tincture of sol and luna, proceeding from the conjunction, or communication of these two, to wit, the bodies of sol and luna, and our water, and the spirit is the mineral power, or virtue of the bodies, and of the water which carries the soul or white tincture, in or upon the bodies, and also out of the bodies like as the tinctures or colours in dying cloth are by the water put upon, and diffused in and through the cloth. And this mercurial spirit is the chain or band of the solar soul; and the solar body is that body which contains the spirit and soul, having the power of fixing in itself, being joined with luna. The spirit therefore penetrates, the body fixes, and the soul joins together, tinges and whitens. From these three bodies united together is our stone made; to wit, sol, luna, and mercury.

24. Therefore with this our golden water, a natural substance is extracted, exceeding all natural substances; and so, except the bodies be broken and destroyed, imbibed, made subtile and fine, thriftily, and diligently managed, till they are abstracted from, or lose their grossness or solid substance, and be changed into a subtile spirit, all our labour will be in vain. And unless the bodies be made no bodies or incorporeal, that is converted into the philosophers mercury, there is no rule of art yet found out to work by. The reason is, because it is impossible to draw out of the bodies all that most thin and subtile spirit, which has in itself the tincture, except it first be resolved in our water. Dissolve then the bodies in this our golden water, and boil them until all the tincture is brought forth by the water, in a white colour and a white oil; and when you see this whiteness upon the water, then know that the bodies are melted, liquified, or dissolved. Continue then this boiling, till the dark, black, and white cloud is brought forth, which they have conceived.

25. Put therefore the perfect bodies of metals, to wit, sol and luna, into our water in a vessel, hermetically sealed, upon a gentle fire, and digest continually, till they are perfectly resolved into a most precious oil. Saith Adfar, digest with a gentle fire, as it were for the hatching of chickens, so long till the bodies are dissolved, and their perfectly conjoined tincture is extracted, mark this well. But it is not extracted

52

all at once, but it is drawn out by little and little, day by day, and hour by hour, till after a long time, the solution thereof is completed, and that which is dissolved always swims atop. And while this dissolution is in hand, let the fire be gentle and continual, till the bodies are dissolved into a viscous and most subtile water, and the whole tincture be educed, in colour first black, which is the sign of a true dissolution.

26. Then continue the digestion, till it become a white fixed water, for being digested in balneo, it will afterwards become clear, and in the end become like common argent vive, ascending by the spirit above the first water. When there you see bodies dissolved in the first viscous water, then know, that they are turned into a vapour, and the soul is separated from the dead body, and by sublimation, turned into the order of spirits. Whence both of them, with a part of our water, are made spirits flying up in the air; and there the compounded body, made of the male and female, viz. of sol and luna, and of that most subtile nature, cleansed by sublimation, taketh life, and is made spiritual by its own humidity. That is by its own water; like as a man is sustained by the air, whereby from thenceforth it is multiplied, and increases in its own kind, as do all other things. In such an ascention therefore, and philosophical sublimation, all are joined one with another, and the new body subtilized, or made living by the spirit, miraculously liveth or springs like a vegetable.

27. Wherefore, unless the bodies be attenuated, or made thin, by the fire and water, till they ascend in a spirit, and are made or do become like water and vapour or mercury, you labour wholly in vain. But when they arise or ascend, they are born or brought forth in the air or spirit, and in the same they are changed, and made life with life, so as they can never be separated, but are as water mixed with water. And therefore, it is wisely said, that the stone is born of the spirit, because it is altogether spiritual. For the vulture himself flying without wings cries upon the top of the mountain, saying, I am the white brought forth from the black, and the red brought forth from the white, the citrine son of the red; I speak the truth and lie not.

28. It sufficeth thee then to put the bodies in the vessel, and into the water once and for all, and to close the vessel well, until a true separation is made. This the obscure artist calls conjunction, sublimation, assation, extraction, putrefaction, ligation, desponsation, subtilization, generation, etc.

53

29. Now the whole magistery may be perfected, work, as in the generation of man, and of every vegetable; put the seed once into the womb, and shut it up well. Thus you may see that you need not many things, and that this our work requires no great charges, for that there is but one stone, there is but one medicine, one vessel, one order of working, and one successive disposition to the white and to the red. And although we say in many places, take this, and take that, yet we understand, that it behoves us to take but one thing, and put it once into the vessel, until the work be perfected. But these things are so set down by obscure philosophers to deceive the unwary, as we have before spoken; for is not this "ars cabalistica" or a secret and a hidden art? Is it not an art full of secrets? And believest thou O fool that we plainly teach this secret of secrets, taking our words according to their literal signification? Truly, I tell thee, that as for myself, I am no ways self seeking, or envious as others are; but he that takes the words of the other philosophers according to their common signification, he even already, having lost Ariadne's clue of thread, wanders in the midst of the labyrinth, multiplies errors, and casts away his money for nought.

30. And I, Artephius, after I became an adept, and had attained to the true and complete wisdom, by studying the books of the most faithful Hermes, the speaker of truth, was sometimes obscure also as others were. But when I had for the space of a thousand years, or thereabouts, which has now passed over my head, since the time I was born to this day, through the alone goodness of God Almighty, by the use of this wonderful quintessence. When I say for so very long a time, I found no man that had found out or obtained this hermetic secret, because of the obscurity of the philosophers words. Being moved with a generous mind, and the integrity of a good man, I have determined in these latter days of my life, to declare all things truly and sincerely, that you may not want anything for the perfecting of this stone of the philosophers. Excepting one certain thing, which is not lawful for me to discover to any, because it is either revealed or made known by God Himself, or taught by some master, which notwithstanding he that can bend himself to the search thereof, by the help of a little experience, may easily learn in this book.

31. In this book I have therefore written the naked truth, though clothed or disguised with a few colours; yet so that every good and

54

wise man may happily have those desirable apples of the Hesperides from this our philosophers tree. Wherefore praises be given to the most high God, who has poured into our soul of his goodness; and through a good old age, even an almost infinite number of years, has truly filled our hearts with his love, in which, methinks, I embrace, cherish, and truly love all mankind together. But to return to our business. Truly our work is perfectly performed; for that which the heat of the sun is a hundred years in doing, for the generation of one metal in the bowels of the earth; our secret fire, that is, our fiery and sulphureous water, which is called Balneum Mariae, doth as I have often seen in a very short time.

32. Now this operation or work is a thing of no great labour to him who knows and understands it; nor is the matter so dear, consideration how small a quantity does suffice, that it may cause any man to withdraw his hand from it. It is indeed, a work so short and easy, that it may well be called a woman's work, and the play of children. Go to it then, my son, put up thy supplications to God Almighty; be diligent in searching the books of the learned in this science; for one book openeth another; think and meditate of these things profoundly; and avoid all things which vanish in or will not endure the fire, because from those adustible, perishing or consuming things, you can never attain to the perfect matter, which is only found in the digesting of your water, extracted from sol and luna. For by this water, colour, and ponderosity or weight, are infinitely given to the matter; and this water is a white vapour, which like a soul flows through the perfect bodies, taking wholly from them their blackness, and impurities, uniting the two bodies in one, and increasing their water. Nor is there any other thing than Azoth, to wit, this our water, which can take from the perfect bodies of sol and luna, their natural colour, making the red body white, according to the disposition thereof.

33. Now let us speak of the fire. Our fire then is mineral, equal, continuous; it fumes not, unless it be too much stirred up, participates of sulphur, and is taken from other things than from the matter; it overturns all things, dissolves, congeals, and calcines, and is to be found out by art, or after an artificial manner. It is a compendious thing, got without cost or charge, or at least without any great purchase; it is humid, vapourous, digestive, altering, penetrating, subtile, spiritous, not violent, incombustible, circumspective,

55

continent, and one only thing. It is also a fountain of living water, which circumvolveth and contains the place, in which the king and queen bathe themselves; through the whole work this moist fire is sufficient; in the beginning, middle and end, because in it, the whole art does consist. This is the natural fire, which is yet against nature, not natural and which burns not; and lastly, this fire is hot, cold, dry, moist; meditate on these things, and proceed directly without anything of a foreign nature. If you understand not these fires, give ear to what I have yet to say, never as yet written in any book, but drawn from the more abstruse and occult riddles of the ancients.

34. We have properly three fires, without which our art cannot be perfected; and whosoever works without them takes a great deal of labour in vain. The first fire is that of the lamp, which is continuous, humid, vaporous, spiritous, and found out by art. This lamp ought to be proportioned to the enclosure; wherein you must use great judgment, which none can attain to, but he that can bend to the search thereof. For if this fire of the lamp be not measured, or duly proportioned or fitted to the furnace, it will be, that either for the want of heat you will not see the expected signs, in their limited times, whereby you will lose your hopes and expectation by a too long delay; or else, by reason of too much heat, you will burn the "flores auri", the golden flowers, and so foolishly bewail your lost expense.

35. The second fire is ignis cinerum, an ash heat, in which the vessel hermetically sealed is recluded, or buried; or rather it is that most sweet and gentle heat, which proceeding from the temperate vapours of the lamp, does equally surround your vessel. This fire is not violent or forcing, except it be too much excited or stirred up; it is a fire digestive; alterative, and taken from another body than the matter; being but one only, moist also, and not natural.

36. The third fire, is the natural fire of water, which is also called the fire against nature, because it is water; and yet nevertheless, it makes a mere spirit of gold, which common fire is not able to do. This fire is mineral, equal, and participates of sulphur; it overturns or destroys, congeals, dissolves, and calcines; it is penetrating, subtile, incombustible and not burning, and is the fountain of living water, wherein the king and queen bathe themselves, whose help we stand in need of through the whole work, through the beginning, middle, and end. But the other two above mentioned, we have not always

occasion for, but only at sometimes. In reading therefore the books of the philosophers, conjoin these three fires in your judgment, and without doubt, you will understand whatever they have written of them.

37. Now as to the colours, that which does not make black cannot make white, because blackness is the beginning of whiteness, and a sign of putrefaction and alteration, and that the body is now penetrated and mortified. From the putrefaction therefore in this water, there first appears blackness, like unto broth wherein some bloody thing is boiled. Secondly, the black earth by continual digestion is whitened, because the soul of the two bodies swims above upon the water, like white cream; and in this only whiteness, all the spirits are so united, that they can never fly one from another. And therefore the laton must be whitened, and its leaves unfolded, i.e., its body broken or opened, lest we labour in vain; for this whiteness is the perfect stone for the white work, and a body ennobled to that end; even the tincture of a most exuberant glory, and shining brightness, which never departs from the body it is once joined with. Therefore you must note here, that the spirits are not fixed but in the white colour, which is more noble than the other colours, and is more vehemently to be desired, for that as it were the complement or perfection of the whole work.

38. For our earth putrefies and becomes black, then it is putrefied in lifting up or separation; afterwards being dried, its blackness goes away from it, and then it is whitened, and the feminine dominion of the darkness and humidity perisheth; then also the white vapour penetrates through the new body, and the spirits are bound up or fixed in the dryness. And that which is corrupting, deformed and black through the moisture, vanishes away; so the new body rises again clear, pure, white, and immortal, obtaining the victory over all its enemies. And as heat working upon that which is moist, causeth or generates blackness, which is the prime or first colour, so always by decoction more and more heat working upon that which is dry begats whiteness, which is the second colour; and then working upon that which is purely and perfectly dry, it produces citrinity and redness, thus much for colours. We must know therefore, that thing which has its head red and white, but its feet white and afterwards red; and its eyes beforehand black, that this thing, I say, is the only matter of our magistery.

39. Dissolve then sol and luna in our dissolving water, which is

familiar and friendly, and the next in nature to them; and is also sweet and pleasant to them, and as it were a womb, a mother, an original, the beginning and the end of their life. That is the reason why they are meliorated or amended in this water, because like nature, rejoices in like nature, and like nature retains like nature, being joined the one to the other, in a true marriage, by which they are made one nature, one new body, raised again from the dead, and immortal. Thus it behoves you to join consanguinity, or sameness of kind, by which these natures, will meet and follow one another, purify themselves and generate, and make one another rejoice; for that like nature now is disposed by like nature, even that which is nearest, and most friendly to it.

40. Our water then is the most beautiful, lovely, and clear fountain, prepared only for the king, and queen, whom it knows very well, and they it. For it attracts them to itself, and they abide therein for two or three days, to wit, two or three months, to wash themselves therewith, whereby they are made young again and beautiful. And because sol and luna have their original from this water their mother; it is necessary therefore that they enter into it again, to wit, into their mothers womb, that they may be regenerated and born again, and made more healthy, more noble and more strong. If therefore these do not die and be converted into water, they remain alone or as they were and without fruit; but if they die, and are resolved in our water, they bring forth fruit a hundred fold; and from that very place in which they seem to perish, from thence shall they appear to be that which they were not before.

41. Let therefore the spirit of our living water be, with all care and industry, fixed with sol and luna; for that they being converted into the nature of water become dead, and appear like to the dead; from thence afterwards being revived, they increase and multiply, even as do all sorts of vegetable substances; it suffices then to dispose the matter sufficiently without, because that within, it sufficiently disposes itself for the perfection of its work. For it has in itself a certain and inherent motion, according to the true way and method, and a much better order than it is possible for any man to invent or think of. For this cause it is that you need only to prepare the matter, nature herself will perfect it; and if she be not hindered by some contrary thing, she will not overpass her own certain motion, neither in conceiving or generating, nor in bringing forth.

42. Wherefore, after the preparation of the matter, beware only lest by too much heat or fire, you inflame the bath, or make it too hot; secondly, take heed, lest the spirit should exhale, lest it hurt the operator, to wit, lest it destroy the work, and induce many informities, as trouble, sadness, vexation, and discontent. From these things which have been spoken, this axiom is manifest, to wit, that he can never know the necessary course of nature, in the making or generating of metals, who is ignorant of the way of destroying them. You must therefore join them together that are of one consanguinity or kindred; for like natures do find out and join with their like natures, and by putrifying themselves, and mix together and mortify themselves. It is needful therefore to know this corruption and generation, and the natures do embrace one another, and are brought to a fixity in a slow and gentle fire; how like natures rejoiceth with like natures; and how they retain one another, and are converted into a white consistency.

43. This white substance, if you will make it red, you must continually decoct it in a dry fire till it be rubified, or become red as blood, which is nothing but water, fire, and true tincture. And so by a continual dry fire, the whiteness is changed, removed, perfected, made citrine, and still digested till it become to a true red and fixed colour. And consequently by how much more this red is decocted in this gentle heat, by so much more it is heightened in colour, and made a true tincture of perfect redness. Wherefore with a dry fire, and a dry calcination, without any moisture, you must decoct this compositum, till it be invested with a most perfect red colour, and then it will be the true and perfect elixir.

44. Now if afterwards you would multiply your tincture, you must again resolve that red, in new and fresh dissolving water, and then by decoctions first whiten, and then rubify it again, by the degrees of fire, reiterating the first method of operating in this work. Dissolve, coagulate, and reiterate the closing up, the opening and multiplying in quantity and quality at your own pleasure. For by a new corruption and generation, there is introduced a new motion. Thus we can never find an end if we do always work by reiterating the same thing over and over again, viz. by solution and coagulation, by the help of our dissolving water, by which we dissolve and congeal, as we have formerly said, in the beginning of the work. Thus also is the virtue thereof increased, and multiplied both in quantity

59

and quality; so that if after the first course of operation you obtain a hundred fold; by a second fold you will have a thousand fold; and by a third; ten thousand fold increase. And by pursuing your work, your projection will come to infinity, tinging truly and perfectly, and fixing the greatest quantity how much soever. Thus by a thing of easy and small price, you have both colour, goodness, and weight.

45. Our fire then and azoth are sufficient for you: decoct, reiterate, dissolve, congeal, and continue this course, according as you please, multiplying it as you think good, until your medicine is made fusible as wax, and has attained the quantity and goodness or fixity and colour you desire. This then is the compleating of the whole work of our second stone (observe it well) that you take the perfect body, and put it into our water in a glass vesica or body well closed, lest the air get in, or the enclosed humidity get out. Keep it in digestion in a gentle heat, as it were of a balneum, and assiduously continue the operation or work upon the fire, till the decoction and digestion is perfect. And keep it in this digestion of a gentle heat, until it be putrified and re-solved into blackness, and be drawn up and sublimed by the water, and is thereby cleaned from all blackness and impurity, that it may be white and subtile. Until it comes to the ultimate or highest purity of sublimation, and utmost volatility, and be made white both within and without: for the vulture flying in the air without wings, cries out, that it might get up upon the mountain, that is upon the waters, upon which the "spiritus albus" or spirit of whiteness is born. Continue still a fitting fire, and that spirit, which is the subtile being of the body, and of the mercury will ascend upon the top of the water, which quintessence is more white than the driven snow. Continue yet still, and towards the end, increase the fire, till the whole spiritual substance ascend to the top. And know well, that whatsoever is clear, white-pure and spiritual, ascends in the air to the top of the water in the substance of a white vapour, which the philosophers call their virgin milk.

46. It ought to be, therefore, as one of the Sybills said, that the son of the virgin be exalted from the earth, and that the white quintessence after its rising out of the dead earth, be raised up towards heaven; the gross and thick remaining in the bottom, of the vessel and the water. Afterwards, the vessel being cooled, you will find in the bottom the black faeces, scorched and burnt, which separate from the spirit and quintessence of whiteness, and cast them away.

Then will the argent vive fall down from our air and spirit, upon the new earth, which is called argent vive sublimed by the air or spirit, whereof is made a viscous water, pure and white. This water is the true tincture separated from all its black faeces, and our brass or latten is prepared with our water, purified and brought to a white colour. Which white colour is not obtained but by decoction and coagulation of the water; decoct therefore, continually, wash away the blackness from the latten, not with your hands, but with the stone, or the fire, or our second mercurial water which is the true tincture. This separation of the pure from the impure is not done with hands, but nature herself does it, and brings it to perfection by a circular operation.

47. It appears then, that this composition is not a work of the hands, but a change of the natures; because nature dissolves and joins itself, sublimes and lifts itself up, and grows white, being separated from the faeces. And in such a sublimation the more subtile, pure, and essential parts are conjoined; for that with the fiery nature or property lifts up the subtile parts, it separates always the more pure, leaving the grosser at the bottom. Wherefore your fire ought to be gentle and a continual vapour, with which you sublime, that the matter may be filled with spirit from the air, and live. For naturally all things take life from the inbreathing of the air; and so also our magistery receives in the vapour or spirit, by the sublimation of the water.

48. Our brass or latten then, is to be made to ascend by the degrees of fire, but of its own accord, freely, and without violence; except the body therefore be by the fire and the water broken, or dissolved, and attenuated, until it ascends as a spirit, or climbs like argent vive, or rather as the white soul, separated from the body, and by sublimation dilated or brought into a spirit, nothing is or can be done. But when it ascends on high, it is born in the air or spirit, and is changed into spirit: and becomes life with life, being only spiritual and incorruptible. And by such an operation it is that the body is made spirit, of a subtile nature, and the spirit is incorporated with the body, and made one with it; and by such a sublimation, conjunction, and raising up, the whole, both body and spirit are made white.

49. This philosophical and natural sublimation therefore is necessary, which makes peace between, or fixes the body and spirit,

which is impossible to be done otherwise, than in the separation of these parts. Therefore it behoves you to sublime both, that the pure may ascend, and the impure and earthy may descend, or be left at the bottom, in the perplexity of a troubled sea. And for this reason it must be continually decocted, that it may be brought to a subtile property, and the body may assume, and draw to itself the white mercurial soul, which it naturally holds, and suffers not to be separated from it, because it is like to it in the nearness of the first, pure and simple nature. From these things it is necessary, to make a separation by decoction, till no more remains of the purity of the soul, which is not ascended and exalted to the higher part, whereby they will both be reduced to an equality of properties, and a simple pure whiteness.

50. The vulture flying through the air, and the toad creeping upon the ground, are the emblems of our magistery. When therefore gently and with much care, you separate the earth from the water, that is from the fire, and the thin from the thick, then that which is pure will separate itself from the earth, and ascend to the upper part, as it were into heaven, and the impure will descend beneath, as to the earth. And the more subtile part in the superior place will take upon it the nature of a spirit, and that in the lower place, the nature of an earthy body. Wherefore, let the white property with the more subtile part of the body, be by this operation, made to ascend leaving the faeces behind, which is done in a short time. For the soul is aided by her associate and fellow, and perfected by it. My mother, saith the body, has begotten me, and by me she herself is begotten; now after I have taken from her, her flying, she, after an admirable manner becomes kind and nourishing, and cherishing the son whom she has begotten, till he come to a ripe or perfect age.

51. Hear now this secret: keep the body in our mercurial water, till it ascends with the white soul, and the earthy part descends to the bottom, which is called the residing earth. Then you shall see the water to coagulate itself with the body, and be assured the art is true; because the body coagulates the moisture into dryness, like as the rennet of a lamb or calf turns milk into cheese. In the same manner the spirit penetrates the body, and is perfectly comixed with it in its smallest atoms, and the body draws to itself his moisture, to wit, its white soul, like as the loadstone draws iron, because of the nearness and likeness of its nature; and then one contains the other.

And this is the sublimation and coagulation, which retaineth every volatile thing, making it fixed for ever.

52. This compositum then is not a mechanical thing, or a work of the hands, but as I said, a changing of natures; and a wonderful connexion of their cold with hot, and the moist with the dry; the hot is mixed with the cold, and the dry with the moist: By this means is made the mixture and conjunction of body and spirit, which is called a conversion of contrary spirits and natures, because by such a dissolution and sublimation, the spirit is converted into a body and body in a spirit. So that the natures being mingled together, and reduced into one, do change one another: and as the body corporifies the spirit, or changes it into a body, so also does the spirit convert the body into a tinging and white spirit.

53. Wherefore as the last time I say, decoct the body in our white water, viz. mercury, till it is dissolved into blackness, and then by continual decoction, let it be deprived of the same blackness, and the body so dissolved, will at length ascend or rise with a white soul. And then the one will be mixed with the other, and so embrace one another that it shall not be possible any more to separate them, but the spirit, with a real agreement, will be united with the body, and make one permanent or fixed substance. And this is the solution of the body, and coagulation of the spirit which have one and the same operation. Who therefore knows how to conjoin the principles, or direct the work, to impregnate, to mortify, to putrefy, to generate, to quicken the species, to make white, to cleanse the vulture from its blackness and darkness, till he is purged by the fire and tinged, and purified from all his spots, shall be the possessor of a treasure so great that even kings themselves shall venerate him.

54. Wherefore, let our body remain in the water till it is dissolved into a subtile powder in the bottom of the vessel and the water, which is called the black ashes; this is the corruption of the body which is called by the philosophers or wise men, "Saturnus plumbum philosophorum", and pulvis discontinuatus, viz. saturn, latten or brass, the lead of the philosophers, the disguised powder. And in this putrefaction and resolution of the body, three signs appear, viz, a black colour, a discontinuity of parts, and a stinking smell, not much unlike to the smell of a vault where dead bodies are buried. These ashes then are those of which the philosophers have spoken so much which remained in the lower part of the vessel, which we ought not to

undervalue or despise; in them is the royal diadem, and the black and unclean argent vive, which ought to be cleansed from its blackness, by a continual digestion in our water, till it be elevated above in a white colour, which is called the gander, and the bird of Hermes. He therefore that maketh the red earth black, and then renders it white, has obtained the magistery. So also he who kills the living, and revives the dead. Therefore make the black white, and the white black, and you perfect the work.

55. And when you see the true whiteness appear, which shineth like a bright sword, or polished silver, know that in that whiteness there is redness hidden. But then beware that you take not that whiteness out of the vessel, but only digest it to the end, that with heat and dryness, it may assume a citron colour, and a most beautiful redness. Which when you see, render praises and thanksgiving to the most great and good God, who gives wisdom and riches to whomsoever He pleases, and takes them away according to the wickedness of a person. To Him, I say, the most wise and Almighty God, be glory for ages and ages. AMEN.

5.   The Secrets of Antimony

With the termination of the *Secret Book* by Artephius in Chapter 4, it is well to recall John Pontanus, who informs us that this book is the only one among hundreds of others to speak the truth, and without any equivocation. Pontanus writes, speaking of those who are searching:

> "I wonder not that so many, and so great men, have not attained unto the work. They have erred, they do err, and they will err; because the philosophers, *Artephius only excepted*, have concealed the principle or proper agent. And unless I had read Artephius, and sensibly understood his speech I had never arrived to the completement of the work."

Artephius writes in paragraph 31 of his book:

> "I have therefore written the naked truth in this book."

Now the first word that appears in the treatise is antimony, the metal which was rarely mentioned in alchemical literature and, even where noticed, was passed over as though it were of no account. The reader might search in hundreds of alchemical works, and still not come across this metal called antimony. Yet Artephius is so frank that, right at the outset, he makes known to us the secret, that antimony is essential to the work. But he has left the searcher one problem. Artephius writes in paragraph 30:

> "Being moved with a generous mind, I have determined to declare all things truly, and sincerely, that you may not want anything for the perfecting of this stone of the philosophers. Excepting one certain thing, which is not lawful for me to discover, to any, because it is either revealed or made known by God Himself, or taught by some master, which notwithstanding, he that can bend

65

himself to the search thereof, by the help of a little experience, may easily learn in this book" (and this is the secret fire of Pontanus).

In this last sentence, Artephius speaks true, for in the treatise he mentions "the red servant", which is the key to the mystery. Thus we are presented with a beautiful castle, which has the one and only path to it blocked, but there is a way to clear this path.

A line from one of the many books by Thomas Vaughan often caused the present writer much thought, and it supplies the key that fits. The line is: "to think, that an iron key should be the means to open a treasury of gold". And so, it may be inferred, iron is the metal which is also essential to antimony in alchemical work—and yet is never mentioned in his book.*

It was earlier explained that in the alchemical art, the first step is to amalgamate certain metals; not in the usual manner as carried out in metallurgy, but dissolved and liquefied into their smallest components or elements, so that when mixed, it is no easy matter to restore them into the original form, and this process can so change their condition that an entirely new metal or powder is formed. Now it was found that antimony can help to facilitate this. Professor Hermann Boerhaave, a famous Dutch doctor and scientist who lived from 1668 to 1738, when writing on the subject of alchemy, wrote the following with regard to antimony (which by the way is in exact agreement with Artephius):

"The term 'Menstruum' seems to have had its rise thus: Lully and other ancient chemists observing the most kindly solutions to be

* Further, it is quite revealing to compare the physical and chemical qualities of antimony with the passages in treatises which deal with the preparation of "our mercury". Antimony is obtained from the sulphide known as stibnite by heating it with scrap iron, which removes the sulphur. This perhaps throws light on why iron was a very necessary catalyst in the preparation of "our mercury".

There are three forms of antimony: a grey lustrous crystalline metal, a black powder like soot which acquires a metallic lustre when polished (this is obtained when antimony is precipitated chemically), an unstable yellow form, and finally an explosive amorphous form which has a silvery colour and which explodes if dropped or heated to 100°C. Obviously when experimenting with antimony, the experimenter should be very careful of the last form.

Although most forms of antimony are poisonous it is still used in some modern medicines, these uses providing an indication of its possible action in the "elixir of life".

66

made by digestion with a heat no greater than that of the human body, in about 42 days, they termed this space of time a philosophical month, and the solvent employed a menstruum intimating that the body performed the dissolution by a menstrual digestion. This term indeed, was first appropriated to the solvent for the philosophers' stone, but it afterwards came to be applied generally to all solvents. All minerals of a metalline nature are solid menstrua, and especially antimony which dissolves metals with as much ease as fire thaws ice. But there is no method yet known of recovering the metals with which antimony has once been fused: all of them including gold, being lost in copellation therewith, which furnishes reason to suspect that it destroys the metalline form. This is certain, that nothing is better suited to alter the nature of metals than antimony. Whence I cannot but suspect that the adepts made use of antimony as a menstruum in the preparation of their stone: Nor do I believe there is a better way to obtain the secret. At least, were I to go in quest of it, I should willingly begin my enquiries with this property of antimony."

Here is confirmation of the importance of antimony in the art of alchemy. Boerhaave tells us that most metals will fuse with antimony permanently, including gold. Although Artephius has not mentioned iron, many adepts have claimed that iron is an essential ingredient; therefore we may assume that in the works of the philosophers, antimony and iron are essential to bring success in the art. Among other claims, it has been said that iron is fiery in nature, and in conjunction with gentle antimony it will bring about the desired end. Thus we now have two ingredients, yet note that these two when dissolved and fused together into a Regulus,* are counted as *one* ingredient or principle. Now the consensus of adepts always said that only *three* principles were used to produce the Stone. The third principle is not a metal, but we need three metals and, although the "Secret Fire" is used, remember the "Secret Fire" is not accounted a metal. Sol therefore takes the place of the "Secret Fire"—as a metal.

We must now return to Artephius for the mercury we require. In paragraph 3, Artephius has told us:

* A metallic compound—the word being derived from *regis*, king.

"The whole then of this antimonial secret is, that we know by it to extract or draw forth argent vive, out of the body of magnesia (the compound or regulus) not burning, and this is antimony and a mercurial sublimate. That is, you must extract a living and incombustible water . . ." [Magnesia is the alchemists name for the metallic compound or regulus, and the mercurial sublimate is always referred to as water; often they call it vinegar.]

Later in paragraph 4 he says:

". . . and therefore without this our antimonial vinegar, the aurum album of the philosophers cannot be made. And because in our vinegar, there is a double substance of argentum vivum, the one from antimony and the other from mercury sublimated; it does give a double weight and substance of fixed argent vive."

Herein then, in this substance known as "our Mercury", which is a mercurial sublimate, a vapour of metals, it would appear, the greatest secret of alchemy lies deeply buried, and may only be unearthed by the empirical method of trial and error. This salt, this aurum album or white gold, as they have called it, is the base we have to find before one can proceed, for obviously after what has been said above, ordinary quicksilver is of no use in the creation of the Philosophers' Stone.

Here in the following quotations from several alchemical treatises, a variety of statements on the subject is presented: these may just present a few more hints to lead the researcher to the truth.

Geber:

"Praised be the Most High who has created 'our mercury', and has given it a nature overcoming all things."

Philalethes:

" 'Our mercury' is the salt of the wiseman, without which, whoever operates, is like an archer who shoots without a bow-string, and yet it is nowhere to be found on earth, but is formed by us, not by creation, but by extracting it out of those things in which it is, nature co-operating in a wonderful manner, by a witty art."

And a little further on, Philalethes says:

"As flesh is generated from coagulated blood, so gold is generated out of coagulated mercury."

Bernard Trevisan affirms that:

"Gold is nothing but quicksilver congealed by its sulphur."

And in another place he writes:

"The solvent differs from the soluble only in proportion and degree of digestion, but not in matter, since nature has formed the one out of the other without any addition, even by a process, equally simple and wonderful, she evolves gold out of quick-silver."

Again:

"The sages have it that gold is nothing but quicksilver perfected and digested in the bowels of the earth, and they have signified that this is brought about only by sulphur, which coagulates the mercury, and digests it by its own heat. Hence the sages have said, that gold is nothing but mature quicksilver."

The Sound of the Trumpet gives forth in no uncertain tones:

"Extract quicksilver from the bodies, and you have above ground quicksilver and sulphur of the same substance of which gold and silver are made in the earth."

In the *Art of Alchemy* we read:

"All the sages agree that metal is generated from the vapour of sulphur and mercury."

The effect of reading all the above quotations is to impress the student that his first work is to discover this well-hidden secret: the art of extracting Philosophers' mercury from metals, rather than using the crude mercury we know. The task is to produce vapour from certain metals, which vapour must carry up with it all the elements of the dissolved metallic bodies, and which entering them again will change them into so powerful a metallic catalyst, that gold and silver may be dissolved in it. In fact, it will then be a powder, red for the transmutation into gold, and white for changing into silver. Either of these last two may be used for the preparation of the principles required to begin experiments. So that now three metals have been mentioned: antimony, iron, gold or silver, the latter two never worked together.

One more fact must be known, and it is that the metals must be aided by a catalyst in the first process, and this catalyst must be a liquid, a nitrate salt. Artephius, along with other masters, has spoken of a water, the mercurial sublimate. But this in indeed another water, and is mentioned in paragraph 2 of Artephius. Pontanus also speaks of it, and says that it is "*not of the matter*", which means that it is not a metal or a mineral. The student can now understand why the art of making gold has rarely been found out!

Artephius speaks of three different fires to be used in the art, but actual fire is not used, but ordinary heat is one fire, "our mercury" is another, and the water mentioned in the "Sophic Fire" is the third, because of the power it has of burning, calcinating, or bringing changes about.

Here are some of the names applied to the Philosophers' mercury, culled from many treatises. The descriptive names should hint of the virtues of "our mercury", and be of help in the mystery of its production. It has been called:

"The spirit; the spirit of life; the water of life; the water of our sea; the mineral water; burning water; ardent water. The fire; the secret fire; fire against nature; the invisible fire; our fire; the fire of snowy whiteness; a fire continuous; digesting, not violent, subtile, inclosed, aerial, surrounding, altering, yet not burning, clear, close, circulating, penetrating and alive. The mover; the first agent; philosophical vitriol; that subtle nature cleaned by sublimation; the fat of the mercurial wind; our mercurial water; the second sophic mercury; the venomous fiery dragon; Medea, Theseus who had black sails to his ship; the 'unhappy spring' in *Ripley*

Revived; the porter or servant of Count Bernard; Artephius's 'lamp fire'; the eagles; the vulture of Hermes; the priest. It is called venus, the nymph venus, born of the froth of the ocean; because of the marine acid which enters into the composition of 'the matter of our sea', which acid is the alchemists 'Universal Lunar Mercury'."

(This last sentence is really the catalyst, a key to the whole work, without which no start can be made, and which is not mercury of any kind, but indeed acid; in fact the nitrate spoken of in the last paragraph, is sometimes called vinegar. In practice all that is required is a pure *muriate* or *oxymuriate*.)

From the thousands of names that have been written in treatises to hide the nature of this mysterious "sophic fire", here are a few more from which the perspicacious might pick out some useful indications.

"They call it heaven, celestial water and rain, parting water, aqua (water) regis, a corrosive aqua forte, sharp vinegar, growthful green juice, a growing mercury, a viridescent water, the green lion, *quicksilver (on no account use this)*, menstruum, blood, urine, horsepiss, milk, virgin's milk, white arsenick, sulphureous vapouring and smokey, a fiery burning spirit, a deadly poison piercing and killing all, serpent, dragon, a scorpion devouring his children, a hellish fire, a sharp salt, salammoniac, common salt, an eagle, vulture, bird of Hermes, a melting and calcining furnace", birds, beasts, herbs, juices.

Every one of these names has been used, but until the preparation of this "secret fire" is achieved one cannot even commence the work of alchemy. This is the only ingredient whose name was hidden by *all* the philosophers.

"The philosophers' mercury when made is a brilliantly clear water; it is so clear in appearance that one might be tempted to drink it, but beware, for it is a quick poison, which contains an extract from all the metals used. When mixed with them it becomes a lovely green, and this is known in alchemy as the Green Lion".

71

The "Red Lion", the colour of blood, comes from this same pure water when the metals it is mixed with turn into a bloody appearance, some time after melting. This usually arises when philosophers' mercury is mixed with sol (gold) and other metals.

Finally, here is an extract from a *Summary of Philosophy*, a short treatise written by Nicholas Flamel, in 1409. It is a short description of this mysterious mercury and what it can do.

"This is the right and subtle mercury of the philosophers, which you are to take, which will make the first white work, and then the red. If you have well understood me, both of them are nothing else, as they term them, but the practice, which is so easy and so simple, that a woman sitting by her distaff, may perfect it. As if in winter, she would put her eggs under a hen, without washing them, and no more labour is required about them, than that they should be every day turned, that the chickens may be better and sooner hatched; concerning which enough is said."

Additional proofs of the use of antimony and iron in the alchemical works of Jacob Behmen follow. This work finally sets forth and summarises the preparation and use of the "mercury" derived from antimony through the catalytic action of iron.

PRIMAL MATTER or FIRST PRINCIPLES
by Jacob Behmen (Abridged)

"There is nothing in nature capable of qualifying matter to be harmonised, but one mineral spirit, the ore of which is equal in attraction and repulsion, and the pure metal in a star-like circle of irradiated circulation. Antimony, purified by iron and pounded fine, might be circulated, that is digested to a perfect harmony of the principles. But in the fusion of its purification it has lost the original

72

proportion of its subtle spirit. In order to restore it, use fresh powder. Digest in a long neck flask, three months at blood heat, three months at fever heat, and three months at water boiling heat by a thermometer. If the moisture is scanty, the process will fail as a plant without rain; if the powder is too wet, it will be a long time drying up, and the vessel may burst by the heat rarefying the moisture.

"The matter should fill one-fourth of the glass, and is called the earth; the empty part is the heaven, in which the circulation is performed, harmonising the dense attraction of the fixed, with the subtle repulsion of the volatile parts, and in consequence of its original irradiation in its crude state, it is now capable of a superior irradiation—from the same cause, which is the ethereal fire of the spiritual gas or vapour of antimony ascending and descending, going round inside the glass, piercing the fixity of the earth, and obtaining fixation for itself.

"The action in the retort imitates nature which distils the mineral spirit in the chasms of the globe by a moderate heat. The invisible universal mercury passes into suitable earth and forms metallic ores; —the action in the sealed flasks is like nature under the rocky roof of the mine, which retains the sublimation and reverberates it until it coagulates into metal.

"The agent of the work is the invisible mercury, which is the gas, spirit, or air of antimony, excited in a steady sand-heat as warm as blood. *Various methods will arrive at the same end if this agent is not omitted.* Some of these methods in the hands of an experienced adept are less liable to accidental mischances than the former.

"For instance, an unintermitting distillation of the gas will impregnate and open the powder to solution in the form of water, which will partly or wholly dissolve fresh powder, according to the proportion. By continual abstraction or cohobated distillation from the residuum, it acquires permanency, and when a bright clear water is separated, the residuum yields a red oil in a stronger fire, and leaves a black residuum, which may be calcined to a white fixed earth.

"Fresh antimony in powder will unite easier and safer with these together than with the first gas or water, and the time lost in distilling is saved in digesting. The white water easily absorbs the white fixed earth, and then unites sooner with the red oil by digestion.

"The powder of antimony fixes in digestion sooner with the thick permanent white water of antimony than it would with the volatile

73

clear bright water. It digests rapidly with the red oil, which contains a large proportion of the invisible mercury in a permanent and nearly fixed state of action.

"The calcined white earth made of the residuum of these white and red mercuries contains no mercury and is therefore only fit for union with the said mercuries in some of their various degrees of volatility, and is the best magnet for condensing the first gas.

"The simple work first described performs all these separations virtually in the sealed glass; the other varieties of separation afford permanency to the disolvent, or vehicle which contains the prime agent, so as to allow intervals for its application to various purposes. *No process can finally fail where the invisible universal mercury, or spiritual air of antimony is present—condensed in its proper vehicle in any of the degrees of its permanency.*

"The principle of the work is the power of harmonising the three-fold discordent principles of attraction, repulsion, and circulation. In three months circulation by digestion, the powder is completely black; the opposition of attraction and repulsion ceases; the attraction of the fixed which produced the repulsion of the volatile is slain by the circulation which also dies itself, and all three enter into rest. There is no more compression or expansion, ascent or descent; it has all sunk down black and motionless.

"The same three principles gradually assume a new life, infinitely more powerful in virtue, but without any violent contest, and in three months further, the mild action of the principles in harmony have produced a brilliant whiteness in the matter, which in three months more, becomes a brilliant yellow, red, or purple.

"Every other metal labours after this perfection in vain. Nothing can attain the union that the fiery spirit of antimony forms between the extremes. This spirit of antimony is so full of life, either in its oil or watery form, that if the process fails at any stage, an addition of the spirit will renew it. The white and red powder is increased tenfold in strength and quality by each digestion of it with fresh antimony in powder wet with gas, water or oil of antimony as at first. Each digestion is made in tenfold shorter time than the former, from a few weeks to a few hours.

"The prime matter is antimony purified by iron, and finely pounded. The invisible mercury is the spiritual air of antimony which combines with vegetable or animal fluids, and the solids in its spiritual or watery form, and from thence, combines with metals and stones. From this, the affinities may be learned for practice. The gas will not unite easily with metals or minerals, until it is embodied for that purpose. This may be done either with the *thick red or white mercuries, which are the oil or water of antimony as described.* By circulating, that is digesting the impregnated liquid two months, the gas floats as an oil on weak liquids, or is united with the strong, subduing their corrosion. In these states, it is able to make extracts from or unite with the solids in the three kingdoms, according to the quality to which it was united. These solutions are more powerful and rapid than those with the unctuous water or oil of antimony, but require great skill and experience of the sophic fire."

6. The Green Lion

It is said of "our mercury", the artificial mercury, that gold will dissolve in it as ice in warm water, but the gold takes a long time, possibly a year, before this takes place. It is also called the "dry water which will not wet the hand", and this because it arises as a vapour when it is extracted from metals, and naturally distills into a liquid when it is cooled.

Before considering further quotations from a few treatises which bear out what has been outlined in previous chapters, it is as well to investigate some more rather difficult terminology. Prepared mercury is the vapour of metals, and extracted from antimony and iron.

Saturn, the planetary name given to lead in the old days, was *never* used to describe the metal. It is a blind designed to mislead, and invented owing to its descriptively dark nature. The first change the compound undergoes is that it becomes black in forty days or more (90 days are optimum). But if this colouring was due to lead, nothing will come of the experiment. Also note that antimony is not mentioned at all, but Mars (the name given for iron) is mentioned.

Now to deal with the problem as to whether Venus (or copper) is to be used in the work of preparing the "Secret Fire".

Many alchemical adepts said that Venus is of no use for the purposes of alchemy, and looked upon it with contempt. But Philalethes claims that without Venus nothing will be achieved. We quote from his poem *The Marrow of Alchemy*. (Remember Saturn is really antimony, Mars iron, and the sun gold.)

> Mars is the stout and valiant god of war,
> His body vile, and little is esteemed,
> He's fierce of courage, conquering near & far
> all sturdy opposites, and may be deemed,
> that his rough outside hidden doth enclose,
> a spirit whose full virtue no man knows.

Venus, the planet fair, the god of love,
Whose beauty the stout god of war allures,
her central salt; whoso has wit to prove,
shall find a key all secrets which assures
the owner for to find; I say no more,
for this disclosed by none, hath been before.

To Saturn, Mars with bonds of love is tied,
who is by him devoured of mighty force,
whose spirit Saturn's body doth divide,
and both combining yield a secret source,
from whence doth flow a water wondrous bright,
In which the sun doth set and lose its light.

The "bonds of love" which must be joined as a preliminary work indicate the use of Venus (copper) to join the regulus of Saturn (antimony) and Mars (iron). More detail from Philalethes:

58. But of this mercury, if you desire,
the secret for to learn, attend to me,
for this is a water which yet is fire,
which conquers bodies from their fixed degree,
and makes them fly much like a spirit pure,
this after fixing all flame to endure.

60. Tis Saturn's offspring who a well doth keep,
in which cause Mars to be drowned, then
let Saturn in this well behold his face,
which will seem fresh, young and tender, when
the souls of both are thus together blended,
for each by the other needs to be amended.

61. Then Lo—a star into this well shall fall,
and with its lustrous rays the earth shall shine,
Let venus and her influence withal,
for she is nurse of this stone divine,
The bond of all crystalline mercury
This is the spring in which our sun must die.

62. This is the lunar juice, this is our moon,
This is the Hesperion garden, happy they,

who know it to prepare, for they very soon,
may climb the mountain tops, where day
shall banish darkness and all obscurity.

The sun is gold, and the moon is a name for silver—but silver is not meant here because gold and silver may *never* be used together. The compound or regulus of antimony and iron is often called "mercury" or *luna* to mislead.

Further from *First Principles* by Jacob Behmen:

"This shows the theory of nature in relation to its spirit and to the matter of every sort; the prime matter is antimony purified by iron, and finely pounded; the invisible mercury is the spiritual air of antimony, which combines with animal or vegetable fluids, and then solids, in its spiritual or watery form, and from thence, combines with metals or stones. From this theory, the affinities may be learned for practice. The gas will not unite easily with metals or minerals until it is embodied for that purpose. This may be done either by the thick red or white mercuries, which are the oil and water of antimony. . ."

In alchemical literature, one will often come across the expression, "the red man and his white wife"; and here we may gather what they are. Iron is the red man and antimony is the white wife. Later we can infer that gold is the red man and the regulus is the white wife. Again, the regulus of antimony and iron becomes one principle, the red man, and mercury (which is clear white) is the white wife. All this is useful to know, although not essential, if one is reading the artful philosophers who try to hide their knowledge from dilettantes. But it is well to know that the regulus of antimony and iron is referred to as *one* principle; gold or silver (note that we say *or* silver as these must *not* be used together) is another principle, and mercury is a third, making three principles in all. In many books of the alchemists, they advise that only three principles are to be used, so always remember these three given here. The prepared mercury, of course, is not a metal at all, but is the catalyst, and only called a principle to mislead.

One more confirmation of the ingredients of the regulus of antimony and iron, which will produce "our mercury", this time

79

from the book called *Vade Mecum*. Again, the notes in brackets are comment by the author.

"A crude immature and coagulated Mercury vive, not yet fixed, is the destroyer of the perfect bodies [gold or silver], for truly it destroys them, incrudates and softens them, and renders them fit for our work. It is the offspring of Saturn [Saturn here is not lead, but the appearance of the black stage], and is acknowledged as such by the philosophers, and is the only and greatest secret in the art.

It is necessary that it [the antimony] be freed from all superfluous and burning sulphur with which it is joined in the mine [being found in the natural state as stibnite, a sulphide], after which that which lies hidden in the centre thereof will be manifested. . . . The sign of its [raw state] right preparation is a beautiful whiteness, like the purest silver, a heavenly brightness and a wonderful glittering on the face of its fractures, like the polish of a bright sword.

Ripley calls it the 'green lion' [the main colour of the water which arises in the work from antimony], which devoured the sun. . . . In the *Turba Philosophorum* it is called sea water, in which 'the perfect body' [gold] is decocted until it [the sea water] is congealed. Artephius calls it the most sharp vinegar of the mountains. . . . It is the offspring of old Saturn [remember antimony used to be considered a form of lead], for which reason it has by some been called 'Venus' [see the myths concerning the birth of Venus], and principally for this reason; because she has been connected with the warlike Mars, and has been caught by Vulcan [vulcan is heat] in the act [iron is added in preparing the regulus]. It has been called a 'Wood' and has received the name of 'Diana'. It is likewise called the philosophical mercury . . . and by Artephius a middle substance, because neither a mineral [crude Antimony at this point in the work]. It is moreover a 'middle substance' between the body [gold] and the spirit [secret fire], between earth and water."

Enough has now been said to confirm that antimony and iron are the metals that produce a "mercury" required in the making of our stone. These two when fused into a regulus are the one principle that is called mercury or sometimes luna. Now we require "sulphur", and although most treatises of the art refuse to say where this comes from, the truth is that only gold and silver represent the "sulphur". If there is any doubt about that, study the extract given above from the *Vade Mecum*, and take it for granted. Now we need salt; that is truly a liquid, a burning water, the sea water from the quotation above. This is the "Secret Fire", the catalyst, which is easy to discover, but which no book ever mentions, but enough has been said.

THE SECRET KNOWLEDGE OF MERCURY

The identification of each kind of mercury is one of the deepest secrets in alchemy. It is therefore important to obtain a definite knowledge of what that mercury is, and what that is, mentioned in every case where the name mercury appears in treatises. Sometimes it is "The Philosophers mercury", and at other times, common, vulgar, or ordinary mercury, it is always necessary to notice the manner in which each is said to react upon bodies. From this it may be gathered that there are two kinds of mercury. Both are volatile and liquid in form, but one is a metal, and does not wet the hand, and the other is a liquid which will naturally do so.

It is said of them, common mercury is silvery and opaque, and the philosophers mercury is not a metal, and is clear; as clear as the tears of the eyes, a beautifully clear, brilliant, and shining water, yet by no means a water, rain or dew as it has been described.

When the salt of the philosophers mercury is dissolved in common mercury, the clearness disappears, and it becomes milky and opaque. This is the milk often mentioned. Here it should be reminded that common mercury only becomes clear and transparent by being dissolved in an acid but acid is never used in alchemy so it is seen that both kinds of mercury are opposite in nature.

The philosopher's mercury first arises as a vapour, and is extracted from all metals, but it is undetermined a simple, and not a compound substance. Philalethes says: "For this thing is not water otherwise than to the sight". And the artful sages have said: neither can we

81

imagine that water can be in solid metals. Of course not, but they go on to say and agree too, that there is a despised and common substance from which, although difficult to prepare, yet with little trouble and expense may be obtained the philosophers mercury, also sulphur and salt, the same as in gold and silver. So we have to learn what the philosophers mercury is, called the mercury of the bodies; and common mercury which is the mercury of metals. The latter is only to be used after the former is made.

7. The Red Man and his White Wife

The special treatise and most important work for reference which is given in full in this book, is Artephius; if one studies it closely it will be found to be full of information; every line of it is composed with a deliberate purpose. Supplementary to this work however are the following useful writings extracted from treatises by famous adepts in alchemy: such men as Roger Bacon, Philalethes, and others.

"If you prudently desire to make our elixir, you must extract it from a mineral root. Sulphur and mercury are the mineral roots, and natural principles, upon which nature herself acts and works in the mines and the caverns of the earth. Of them is produced a vapour or cloud, which is the substance and body of metals united. In the same manner, Sol, which is our sulphur, being reduced into mercury by mercury, which is the viscous water made thick, and mixed with its proper earth, by a temperate decoction and digestion, ariseth the vapour. When this vapour is returned into the earth, out of which it is drawn, and in every way spreads through or is mixed with it, as its proper womb, it becomes fixed. Thus the wise man does that by art in a short time, which nature cannot perform in less than a thousand years. Yet notwithstanding, it is not we who make the metals, but nature herself does it.

"Choose then the natural minerals, for nature generates metalline bodies of the vapours of these, or fumes of sulphur and mercury (regulus of antimony and iron), to which all philosophers agree. Know therefore the principles upon which art works, for he who knows not these things shall never attain to the perfection of the work. The second principle of our stone is called mercury, which word stone is a simple name. One philosopher said, this stone is no stone, but that without which, nature never performs anything; which enters into, or is swallowed up by other bodies; and also swallows them up. This is simply argent vive which contains the essential power. For it is the root of metals, harmonizes with them, and is the medium which conjoins the tinctures.

"Euclid advises to work in nothing but in sol and mercury; which joined together, make the wonderful and admirable philosophers' stone. White and red both proceed from one root, no other bodies coming between them. But yet gold, wanting mercury, is hindered from working according to his power. Therefore, know that no stone, or other foreign thing belongs to this work. You must therefore labour the solution of the citrine body to reduce it into its first matter. For we dissolve gold so it may be reduced into its first matter, or nature and that is into mercury. For being broken and made one, they have in themselves the whole tincture both of the agent and patient. Wherefore, make a marriage, that is a conjunction between the red man and his white wife, and you have the whole secret.

"If you marry the white woman to the red man, they will be conjoined and embrace one another, and become impregnated. By themselves they are dissolved, and by themselves they bring forth what they have conceived, whereby the two are made one body. And truly our dissolution is only reducing the hard body into a liquid form, and into the nature of argent vive that the saltness of the sulphur may be diminished. Without our brass then be broken, ground, and gently and prudently managed, till it be reduced from its hard and dense body, into a thin and subtle spirit, you labour in vain.

"He that prudently draws the virtue out of sol, and his shadow, shall obtain a great secret. Again it is said, without sol and his shadow, no tinging virtue or power is generated. And whosoever it is that shall endeavour to make a tinging or colouring tincture without these things, and by any other means, he errs, and goes astray from truth, to his own hurt, loss and detriment.

"The vessel for our stone is one, in which the whole magistery or elixir is performed and perfected; this is a flask whose bottom is round like an egg, smooth within, that it may ascend and descend the more easily. Its largeness ought to be such, that the medicine or matter may not fill above a fourth part of it, made of strong glass, clear and transparent, that you may see through it, all the colours appertaining, and appearing in the work; in which the spirit moving cannot pass or fly away. Let it be so closed that nothing can go out of it, so nothing can enter into it, so that your work will not be spoiled or lost.

"Therefore be very dilligent and careful in the sublimation and liquefaction of the matter, that you increase not your fire too much, whereby the water may ascend to the highest part of the vessel. For then wanting a place of refrigeration, it will stick fast there, whereby the sulphur of the elements will not be perfected. For indeed in this work, it is necessary that they be many times elevated or sublimed, and depressed again. And the gentlest of temperate fires is that only which completes the mixture, makes thick, and perfects the work. Therefore that gentle fire is the greatest and most principal matter of the operation of the elements. Burn our brass with a gentle fire, such as that of a hen for the hatching of eggs, until the body be broken, and the tincture extracted. For with an easy decoction, the water is congealed, and the humidity which corrupteth drawn out; and in drying, the burning is avoided. The happy prosecution of the whole work consists in the exact temperament of the fire; therefore beware of too much heat, for if it be kindled before the time, the matter will be red, before it comes to ripeness and perfection, for that will bring you to despair of attaining the end of your hopes.

"You ought to put on courage, resolution and constancy, in attempting the great work, lest you err and be deceived, sometimes following and doing one thing and then another. For the knowledge of this art does not consist in a great number of things but in unity. Our stone is one, the matter is one, the vessel is one; the government is one, and the whole art and work thereof is one, and begins in one manner, and in one manner it is finished. This is notwithstanding the philosophers have clouded their instructions with enigmatical words and phrases, so that their art may stay hidden.

"Thus they advise to decoct, to commix and conjoin; to sublime, to bake, to grind, to congeal; to make equal, to putrify, to make white and to make red; all of which things, the order, the arrangement, and way of working is all one, which is only to decoct, and therefore to grind is to decoct, of which you are not to be weary. Digest continually, but not in haste, that is with not too great a fire; cease not, or make intermission in your work, follow not the artifice of liars, but pursue your operation to the complement and perfection thereof. Be cautious and watchful, lest your work prove dead or imperfect, and to continue it with a long decoction. Close up well thy vessel and pursue to the end. For there is no generation of things, but by putrefaction; by keeping out the air, and a continual internal motion, with an equal and gentle heat. Remember when you are in your work, all the signs and appearances which arise in every decoction, for they are necessary to be known and understood in order to bring about the perfecting of the matter. You must be sure to be incessant in your operation with a gentle fire to the appearing of the perfect whiteness.

"This then is the thing, that the vessel with the matter be put into heat, so that the middle or one half of the vessel be in the fire, and the other half out of the fire, so that you may daily look into it. And in about the space of 40 days, the superficies or the upper part will appear black as melted pitch; and this is the sign that the citrine body is truly converted into mercury. When you see the blackness of the water to appear, be assured that the body is made liquid. This blackness the philosophers called the first conjunction, the male and female are joined together, and it is the sign of perfect union.

"Yet notwithstanding, the whole tincture is not drawn together; but it goes out every day, by little and little, until by a great length of time, it is perfectly extracted and made complete. And that part of the body which is dissolved, ever ascends or rises to the top, above all the other undissolved matter, which remains yet at the bottom. (Take good notice of what is said in this paragraph, for unless the whole is dissolved into blackness, this first work is incomplete and will lead to failure.)

"In this first decoction, which is called putrefaction, our stone is made all black, to wit, a black earth, by drawing out of its humidity; and in that blackness, the whiteness is hidden. And when the humidity is reverted upon the blackness again, and by a continual soft and gentle digestion is made fixed with its earth, then it becomes white. In this white the redness is hidden; and when it is decocted and digested by the augmentation and continuance of the fire, the earth is changed into redness.

"To return to the black matter in the vessel, continually closed, let this vessel stand continually in the moist fire, till such time as the white appears, like to a white moist salt. This colour is called by the philosophers arsenic, and sal ammoniac, and some have called it, the thing without which no profit is to be had in the work. But whiteness appearing, there is a perfect conjunction of the bodies in this stone, which is then indissoluble. But before it becomes white, you will find many colours to appear. Decoct the male and female together until such time as they shall become one dry body, for except they be dry, the various colours will not appear; for it will ever be black whilst the humidity or moisture has the dominion; but if that be once wasted, then it will emit divers colours after many and several ways.

"And many times it will change from colour to colour, till such time as it comes to the fixed whiteness. But value none of these colours for they are not the true tincture. Yes, many times it becomes citrine and redish, and many times it is dried and becomes liquid again, before the whiteness will appear. Now all this time, the spirit is not perfectly joined with the body, nor will it be perfectly joined but in the white colour. Between the white and the red, again all colours will appear, even to the utmost imagination.

"The matter then of the white and the red among themselves differ not in respect to their essence; but the red needs more subtilization, and longer digestion, and the hotter the fire in the course of operation than the white, because the end of the white work, is the beginning of the red work; and that which is complete in the one is to begin in the other. Therefore without you make the white elixir first, you can never come to the red elixir, that which is indeed the true red. But the heat of this dry fire ought to be double at least to what it was before, and by the help of this fire, the white matter receiveth the admirable tincture of redness.

"You cannot err if you continue the dry fire; therefore with a dry fire, and a dry calcination, decoct the dry matter till it becomes in colour like to vermillion or cinnabar. Decoct the red matter and the more red it is, the more worth it is, and the more decocted it is, the more red it is. Therefore the more decocted, the more precious and valuable the powder will become. Do not cease, though the redness may be somewhat long before it appears. Between the whiteness and the redness, one colour only appears, that is citrine, but it changes from the less to the more, until such time as it is clothed in the purple glory."

What follows is of the greatest importance and is specifically mentioned in Artephius's *Secret Book* in paragraphs 19–20, but here it is taken from an extract from *Root of the World* by Roger Bacon:

"This is a great and certain truth, that the clean ought to be separated from the unclean; for nothing can give that which it has not. For the pure substance is one of simple essence, void of all heterogeneity; but that which is impure and unclean consists of heterogene parts, is not simple, but compounded (to wit of pure and impure) and apt to putrify and corrupt. Therefore let nothing enter into your composition, which is alien or foreign to the matter, as all impurity is; for nothing goes to the composition of our stone, that proceedeth not from it neither in part nor in whole. If any strange or foreign thing be mixed with it, it is immediately corrupted, and by that corruption your work becomes frustrate.

"The citrine bodies, as sol, and etc., you must purge by calcination; and it is then purged or putrified if it be fine and florid. The metal being well cleansed, beat it into fine leaves, and reserve them for use. The white liquor, as mercury, contains two superfluities, which must necessarily be removed from it, viz. its fetid earthiness, which hinders its fusion; and its humidity which causes its flying. The earthiness is thus removed. Put it into a mortar, with its equal weight of pure fine and dry salt, and a little vinegar. Grind all with a pestle, till nothing of the matter appears, but the whole salt becomes very black. Wash this whole matter with pure water till the salt is dissolved; this filthy water decant, put to the mercury again as much more salt and vinegar grinding it as before, and washing it with clean water, which work so often repeat, till the water come clear from it, and that the mercury remains pure bright and clear like a Venice looking glass, and of a celestial colour".

[The beginning of this important paragraph speaks of using only well-purified gold, and in leaf form. Today one may purchase already precipitated gold 99.9 per cent pure, so that the modern scientist is spared this work. From then on, the paragraph deals with the purifying and cleaning Mercury, which of course refers to the regulus of Antimony and Iron, for which a simple recipe is supplied; these two metals may also be bought in the same condition as the gold, and one can be more wasteful with them as the cost is considerably less, although the work is still to be considered, as only when the regulus is made, can the cleaning take place.]

"Then strain it through a linen cloth three or four times doubled into a glass vessel, till it be dry, the proportion of the parts is as 24 to 1. There are 24 hours in a natural day, to which add one, and it is 25 to the rising of the sun. To understand this is wisdom, as Geber saith: 'Endeavour through the whole work to overpower the mercury in commixion', Rhasis saith: 'those bodies come nearest to perfection, which contain the most argent vive.' He further saith: that the philosophers hid nothing but the weight and measure, to wit, the proportions of the ingredients, which is clear, for that none of them all agree one with another therein, which causeth great error. Though the matters be well prepared and well mixed, without the proportions or quantities of the things be just, and according to the reason of the work, you will miss of the truth or the end, and lose all your labour; you will not bring indeed anything to perfection. All this is evident in the examination, when there is a transmutation of the body, or that the body is changed, then let it be put into the cineritium or test, and then it will be consumed, or otherwise remain according as the proportions are more or less just; or just as they ought to be. If they be right and just, according to the reason of that, your body will be incorruptible and remain firm, without any loss, through all essays and trials; you can do nothing in this work without the true knowledge of this thing, whose foundation is natural matter, purity of substance, and right reason or proportion."

From THE MARROW OF ALCHEMY
by Eirenæus Philalethes

I now proceed the practice to discover,
Which weigh with judgement ere you pass it over.

Take then our mercury (which is our Moon)
And it espouse with the terrestial Sun.
Thus man and wife are joined, and to them soon
Add the reviving spirit; this when done
A noble game you soon shall espy, because
You have attended natures noble laws.

Of the Red man one: of the white wife three:
Take thou and mix (which is a good proportion)
Then of the water four parts let there be,

This mixture is our lead, which unto motion
Will be moved, by a most gentle heat,
Which must increased be until it sweat.

But if thou list this pond us to observe,
One of the Sun, two of the moon to take;
In such proportion thou shalt never swerve;
The water let be four, which added up will make
The perfect number, and to thee shall prove
A joyous Sabbath, and the bond of love.

For Latten he is red, but to our work
Availeth not, until he whitened be;
Though in his centre doth a spirit lurk;
Yet appears not, till joined with mercury,
This mercury a tender body is,
The spouse of Sol, whom he doth straightway kiss.

Thus is thy work with trinity begun,
The body and its soul are first conjoined,
And both are with spirit mixed; the Sun,
The Moon, the water, these are one in kind,
In number three, and yet indeed but two,
For why? The sun is hidden, no light doth show.

Two bodies thus combined, we oft do call
Our lead, our brass, and our Hermaphrodite.
Tis red within and fixed, but yet withall,
To sight saturnine, volatile and white.
These separate natures, do not part,
But join, inseparately by our art.

This is the wonder of our hidden work,
That what is perfect we to retrograde
Do cause: Long time to wait, nor does it irk,
Till the water do congeal: this had,
We then sublime, exalt, and fix to dust.
This essence sift, which then revive we must.

For this, in readiness a vial glass,
Oval, or spherical, be sure to have,
In which the matter put, nor out must pass
Ought of the enclosed air, which for to save,
Seal up the neck with a strong seal, and then
The spirits are secure within their den.

So big thy glass let be, as may contain,
Four times at least as much as you enclose,
For vacant space receives the dew and rain,
Which falling down the body doth dispose,
To die and rot, and after to revive,
And to be joined in union, not to strive.

Nor if your glass of too greatness be,
And so the female sperm too much dispersed,
Will not return, this error trust to me,
Thy work will spill, the surest course is best;
Accordingly therefore to your quantity,
In bigness get your glass accordingly.

This is your great rule, if of the woman three,
Then of the man one you take, then equal water
Unto the earth we claim; but if there be
But two to one, then so we mix the matter,
That one more of the spirit doth appear
Than of the body, this by Ripley clear.

We leave the treatises here, and proceed to explain in more detailed form what has been said so far. Generally the time allowed to pass from the white stage to the red stage is five months, and it is said that during this long digestion, hands should not be laid on the vessel. The experimenter would be well advised to experiment with a few vessels so that he can try various combinations of conditions leading to his goal. We have shown by Artephius's book, chapter thirteen, that continual digestion is all that is needed to bring the white to the red stage. But the reader has already been warned many times not to take anything for granted, especially where the adepts in alchemy have been most frank. Therefore the researcher must be on his guard; try moving the vessel in one case, and leaving another to digest undisturbed, observing carefully which brings the best results. But do not open the vessels. Where there is any water in the flask, beware of too much heat, for with the liquid rarefying a weak flask may explode. This is a rule not elsewhere mentioned, but take heed else too much heat will explode a vessel containing wet vapour. More heat can be used where the vapour is not too wet; that is, a metallic vapour.

As the student can never have enough information and instruction to help him, here are more extracts from various treatises on this stage.

First of all from *Ripley Revived* by Philalethes, which describes the work after the white stage has been reached.

"After the white, the fire being continued, the compound will become azure, grey, and then citrine, which will last a long time; and at last end in bloody redness.

"He that supposeth his work ended when the stone is brought to redness is mistaken. But yet again twice turn about thy wheel. The stone by constant and long decoction brought to this pass, anyone who thinketh the race quite run is mistaken. It is a medicine of the first order, and must be brought to third order by imbibitions and cibations, (adding liquid as in the beginning.) which is a second turning round of the wheel; and by fermentation (mixing with pure gold), which is a third turning round of the wheel, which brings the medicine to the third order, and makes it fit for projection. For till the medicine will flow like wax, it cannot enter metals before its flight. Leave not then, where you should begin, but go on till you bring the matter to the third order."

Here is another helpful extract from the same author:

"Consider now thou art in process to a new work, and though in perfect whiteness thy stone was incombustible, yet in continuing it on the fire without moving, it is now become tender again; therefore, although it be not in so great a danger of fire now as heretofore, yet immoderacy now may spoil all; and undo thy hopes.

92

"Govern with prudence therefore during the while that these colours shall come and go, and be not over hasty nor despondent but wait until the end with patience. For in a short time, thou shalt find that this green will be overcome with azure, and that by a pale wan colour, which will at length come to a citrine, which citrine will endure for the space of forty-six days.

"Then shall the heavenly fire descend and illuminate the earth with inconceivable glory. The crown of thy labours shall be brought unto thee, when our Sol shall sit in the south, shining with redness incomparable. This is our Tyre, our basiliske, our red poppy of the rock, our Lion devouring all things. This is our true light, our earth glorified."

The successful adepts in the art each achieved the same end in a variety of ways, and then it followed that if they wrote anything on the subject, they imagined that theirs was the only way. The student is advised not to read much alchemical literature, but to concentrate on selected texts and to try various experiments at the same time. The greatest bugbear of all alchemical work, the time factor, is another reason for trying a number of experiments simultaneously. One must be prepared to be a model of patience and wait for the results without too much handling of the flasks, for we are warned repeatedly that all is nature's work and it is to be carried out without laying on of hands. This makes the work tedious almost to desperation.

The farmer sowing his seed knows exactly what to expect, and therefore can wait on nature patiently, but the tyro in alchemy, not knowing what to expect, can wait many months, never quite knowing if he is on the wrong track or not.

8. The Journey through the Twelve Gates

We may now take up *Ripley Revived*. As mentioned previously in Chapter 2, this is a long poem in twelve parts, which Ripley called his *Twelve Gates*. Here it is presented in an abridged form, omitting many verses which are merely padding, reiteration, or misleading.

When in the work, the three colours are attained, namely black, white, and red, and when the powder is complete, there are still further processes to be carried out. Here Ripley excels, for he deals with all the processes, which most writers have ignored, or mixed up. Ripley deals with each separately, leaving nothing unsaid; he is however very verbose which is the reason for the abridgement.

But let **Ripley** explain his own intention in specifying these twelve gates, which are given in the introduction to his treatise. Although he numbers his gates, it does not necessarily follow that any one should be in correct order.

The first chapter shall be of natural calcination.
The second chapter of dissolution secret and philosophical.
The third chapter of our elemental separation.
The fourth chapter of conjunction matrimonial.
The fifth of putrefaction then shall follow.
Of congealation, albyficate shall be the sixt.
Then of cibation the seventh shall follow next.
The secret of our sublimation, the eight shall show.
The ninth shall be of fermentation.
The tenth of our exaltation, I trow.
The eleventh of our marvellous multiplication.
The twelvth of projection, then recapitulation.
And so this treatise shall take an end.

All this might be compared to making a simple cake in twelve stages or sections; which indeed is not as difficult as it sounds. The materials, type of vessel, proportion, temperature used, signs to look for and time it will take could be arranged according to a similar pattern. Note that the author's comments are in brackets.

THE TWELVE GATES
by Sir George Ripley, 1649 (Abridged)

CALCINATION—The First Gate

Calcination is the purgation of our stone,
Restoring also of his natural heat,
Of radical moisture it looseth none, [metallic vapour]
Inducing solution into our stone most mete. [necessary]
After philosophy I you behight. [advise]
    Do not after the common guise,
      With sulphur and salts prepared in divers wise.

Neither with corrosives, nor with fire alone,
nor with vinegar, nor with water ardent,
neither with the vapour of lead, our stone [do not use lead]
is calcined to our intent;
All they to calcine which so be bent,
    From this hard science withdraw their hand,
      till they our calcining better understand.

For by such calcining, their bodies be shent, [spoiled]
which diminisheth the moisture of our stone;
Therefore when bodies to powder be brent, [burnt]
dry as husks of tree or bone,
of such calx then will we have none;
    For moisture we multiply radical,
      in calcining, deminishing none at all.

Illustrations
from
Atalanta Fugiens

1. A symbolic picture of the alchemical dilemma: how
to gain an entrance to the 'Garden of the Philosophers'.
We see a great gate which is triple locked and barred.
The inside of the garden which is beautiful and orderly
symbolises that the quest is no haphazard affair. The
'Trees of Hermes' are growing there, and water is everywhere visible, even flowing out of the garden to the very
feet of the visitor. Hermes has said that alchemy is an
experiment upon water, and it is worth noting that the
water is named Mercury.

2. The metals are raised from darkness to light.

3. Research must follow in the footsteps of Nature,
with patience and no laying on of hands.

4. The whole art is performed by cooking, care however must be taken not to lose any vapour.

5. Milk, or the Secret Fire or 'Mercury', is the nutriment of all three earthly natures. Antimony reduced to milk, or white earth in liquid.

6. Washing Latona, mother of sun and moon: it must be kept moist like all growing things in nature.

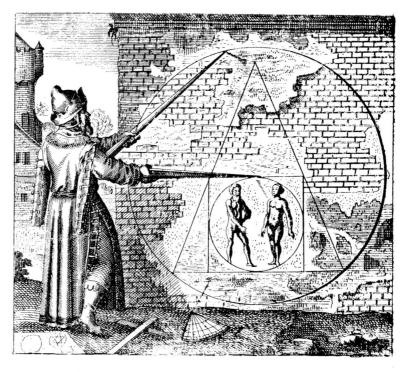

7. Correct proportion is the only method of breaking down the wall of the mystery.

8. Mars and Venus first enter the fire without fear: in this mixture might be shown the first secret from which to prepare Mercury.

9. The search for the 'Golden Fleece' aided by Mars and Mercury.

10. The sun and the moon must copulate as must cock and hen. The moon here does not refer to silver, but to the regulus of antimony and Mars.

11. They must copulate in water to procreate. Everything is done in water which is the Secret Fire or Mercury.

12. Work with two kinds of water, male and female.

13. The Hermes Tree grows in the water. Metals in
process are often seen as leafy shapes.

14. Guard and watch, without the laying on of hands.

15. Father Time is an important ingredient.

16. The rays of sun and moon are never used together in the art of alchemy, and the moon usually refers to the regulus.

17. The symbol of the rising vapours.

18. In heat our water dissolves and reduces all to one kind, but never uncovered as shown here in crude distillation.

19. The green lion with the red lion.

20. The fixed sun and moon strive with the unfixed or black dragon.

21. When the colour citrine is seen, it is the king swimming in the water.

22. Introducing water Mercury to mineral Mercury, 'Sophic Fire' to 'Secret Fire'.

23. Sewing your gold in white earth, in our Mercury. Fermentation is carried out with perfectly fresh gold.

24. The crowned lion. The end of the work.

25. The alchemist may now rest and partake of the
golden apples in the Garden of the Hesperides.

And for a sure ground of our true calcination,
mix wittily kind only with kind,
For kind to kind hath appetite and inclination.
Who knoweth this in knowledge is blind,
he may wander forth as mist in the wind;
 Knowing never with perfectness where to alight,
 because he cannot conceive our words aright.

Join kind with kind therefore as reason is,
for every burgeon answers to his own seed,
man begetteth man, a beast a beast likewise,
further to treat of this is no need,
but understand this point if you wish to speed.
 Everything is first calcined in his own kind,
 This well conceiving, fruit therein shalt thou find.

And we make calx unctous both white and red,
of three degrees, ere our base be perfect;
Fluxible as wax, else stand they in little stead.
By right long process as philosophers write,
A year we take or more for our respite.
 For in less space our calx will not be made.
 Able to teign with colour which will not fade.

As for the proportion thou must beware,
For therein many a one is beguiled.
Therefore thy work that thou not mar, [spoil]
Let thy body be totally filled,
With mercury; As much then so subtiled;
 One of the sun and two of the moon,
 till altogether like pap be done.

(This is a difficult passage. It means one part of the sun or gold, or sulphur, and two parts of the moon (not silver, but our mercury made from antimony and iron). But the mercury is made from three parts of antimony and one of iron. When ready, this is called mercury or moon. Then use only so much liquid to make it into the consistency of pap. This reveals the true proportion, which is one part gold, and two parts what the masters of alchemy called mercury.)

Then make the mercury four to the sun,
Two to the moon as it should be,
And thus thy work must be begun,
in the figure of the trinity:
Three of the body and of the spirit three;
    And for the unity of the substance spiritual,
    one more of the substance corporal.

(In this case the spirit means the water or liquid used to moisten the matter which acts as a catalyst. This verse then means the same as the verse above, with a different wording. The next confusing verse is omitted, and in future, verses of a similar kind will be left out without comment.)

If the water be in proportion to the earth,
With heat in due measure,
Of him shall spring a new burgeon;
both white and red in pure tincture,
which in the fire shall ever endure;
    Kill then the quick, the dead revive,
    Make trinity unity without any strive.

This is the best and surest proportion;
For where is less of the part spiritual, [which means water]
The better therefore shall be solution:
Than if you do it with water small.
Thine earth overglutting which loseth all;
    Take heed therefore to form potter's loam,
    and make you never too wet thy womb.

That loam behold how it tempered is,
The mean how thou it calcinate,
And ever in thy mind, look thou, hear this,
That never thy earth with water be suffocate.
Dry up thy moisture with heat most temperate.
    Help dissolution with moisture of the moon,
    And congealation with the sun, then hast thou done.

But first of thine elements make thou rotation,
and into water thy earth turn first of all;
Then of thy water make air by levitation,
and air make fire. Then master I will thee call,
of all our secrets great and small.
> The wheel of elements thou canst turn about,
> Truly conceiving our writings without doubt.

This done, go backwards, turning thy wheel again,
and into thy water, turn thy fire anon,
and air into earth, else labourest thou in vain,
For so to a temperament is brought our stone,
and natures contrarious, four be made one.
> After they have three times been circulate,
> Also thy base perfectly consumate.

Thus under the moisture of the moon,
and under the temperate heat of the sun,
thy elements shall be incinerate soon,
and then thou hast the mastery won;
Thank God thy work was thus begun.
> For then thou hast one token true,
> Which first in blackness to thee will show.

The head of the crow that token call we,
and some men call it the crow's bill.
Some call it the ashes of Hermes tree,
Our toad of the earth that eateth his fill,
and thus they name after their will.
> Some name it by which it is mortificate,
> The spirit of the earth with venom intoxicate.

But it hath names I say to thee infinite,
For each thing that black is to sight,
named it is till the time that it wax white.
For after blackness when it waxeth bright,
then hath it names of more delight.
> After white things, the red after the same,
> Rule of red things, doth take his name.

99

At the first gate, now thou art in,
of the philosophers castle where they dwell,
Proceed wisely that thou may win,
In at more gates of that castle,
which castle is round as any bell;
>   And gates hath eleven yet mo, [more]
>   One is conquered, now to the second go.

SOLUTION—*The Second Gate*

Of solution now will I speak a word or two,
which showeth out what ere was hid from sight,
and maketh things thin that were thick also;
By the virtue of our first menstrue clear and bright,
In which our bodies have eclipsed been to sight;
>   And of their hard and dry compaction subtilate.
>   Into their own first nature kindly retrograde.

One in gender they be and in number two,
Whose father is the sun, and moon truly is mother,
the mean is mercury, these two and no more,
be our magnesia, our adrop, and none other;
Things there be, but only sister and brother.
>   This is to mean, agent and patient,
>   sulphur and mercury, co-essential to our intent.

Betwixt these two, in quality contrarious,
Engendered is a mean most marvellous,
Which is our mercury and menstrue unctuous;
Our secret sulphur working invisibly,
More fiercely than fire burning the body,
>   Into water dissolving the body mineral,
>   Which night from darkness in the north, we call.

But yet, I trow, thou understandeth not utterly,
The very secret of philosophers dissolution.
Therefore understand me, I councel thee wittily,
For I tell thee truly without delusion,
Our solution is cause of our congealation.

100

For the dissolution on one side corporal,
Causeth congealation on the other side spiritual.

And we dissolve into water which wetteth no hand,
For when the earth is integrally incinerate,
then is the water congealed, this understand;
For the elements be so concatenate,
that when the body from his first form be alterate,
A new form is induced immediately,
For nothing is without form utterly.

And here a secret to thee I will disclose,
which is the ground of our secrets all,
And if thou know it not, thou shalt but lose,
thy labour and costs both great and small,
Take heed therefore in error that thou not fall.
The more thine earth, and the less thy water be,
The rather and better solution shalt thou see.

Behold how ice to water doth relent,
and so it must, for water it was before;
Right so again to water our earth is bent,
and water thereby congealed for ever more,
For after all philosophers which ever was bore, [born]
Every metal was once water mineral,
Therefore with water they turn to water all.

In which water of kind occasionate,
Of qualities been repugnance and diversity,
Things into things must therefore be rotate,
until diversity be brought to perfect unity;
for scripture recordeth when the earth shall be
troubled; and into the deep sea shall be cast,
mountains, our bodies likewise at the last.

Our bodies be likened conveniently
to mountains, which after high planets we name;
Into the deepness therefore of mercury,

101

turn them, and keep thee out of blame;
Then shall you see a noble game.
    How all shall become powder soft as silk,
    So doth our rennet by kind curd our milk.

Then hath our bodies their first form lost,
And others have been induced immediately,
Then hast thou well bestowed thy cost;
Whereas some others uncunningly must go by,
Not knowing the secrets of our philosophy.
    Yet one point more I must tell thee,
    Everybody, know it, hath dimentions three.

Altitude, latitude, and profoundity,
By which always must we turn our wheel.
Knowing thine entrance in the west shall be;
Thy passage forth into north, if thou do well,
And there thy lights shall lose their light each deal,
    For there thou must abide ninety nights,
    In darkness of purgatory without lights.

Then take thy course up to the East anon,
By colours variable passing in manifold wise,
And then be winter and spring nigh overgone;
To the East therefore, thine ascending devise,
For there the sun with daylight uprise;
    In summer, and there disport with delight,
    For there thy work shall become perfect white.

Forth from the East into the south descend,
And set thou up therein thy chariot of fire;
For there is harvest, that is to say an end
Of all thy work after thine own desire;
There shineth the sun up in his own sphere.
    And after the eclipse is in redness with glory,
    As king to reign upon all metals and mercury.

And in one glass must be done all this thing,
Like to an egg in shape and closed well.

Then must you know the measure of firing,
The which unknown thy work is lost each deal,
Let never thy glass be hotter than thou may feel,
    And suffer still in thy bare hand to hold,
    For dread of losing as philosophers have thee told.

Yet to my doctrine furthermore attend,
Beware thy glass thou never open nor move,
From the beginning until thou hast made an end.
If thou do otherwise, thy work may never achieve;
Thus in this chapter which is so brief,
    I have taught thee true solution,
    Now to the third gate go, for this is won.

(Take note, in these last two verses, you are given the size and shape of the flask to use (egg size, 100 to 150 ml. or a shade bigger with a long neck), the measure of the heat ("never thy glass be hotter than thou may feel"), and finally, an instruction not to move or open the glass. But here the experimenter must be wary, and experiment with more than one glass, some bigger, some smaller; some hotter or cooler; some moved or opened, and also some never moved or opened. Watch carefully the results, and take notes. This solution applies to all the processes where the solution is necessary, and remember not to make the matter too wet, as it should always have the consistency of potter's clay, or perhaps slightly wetter.)

SEPARATION—The Third Gate

Separation doth each part from the other divide.
The subtle from the gross, the thick from the thin;
But Manual separation look thou put aside,
For that pertaineth to fools, which little fruit do win.
For in our separation, nature doth not blin. [cease]
    Making division of qualities elemental,
    Into the fith degree till they be turned all.

Earth is turned into water black and blue,
And water after into air under very white,
Air is turned into fire, [red], elements there be no more;

103

Of this is made by craft our stone of great delight.
But of this separation, much more must we write.
    And separation is called by philosophers Definition,
    Of the said elements, tetraptative dispersion.

And of this separation, I find a like figure,
Thus spoken by the prophet, in the psalmody;
God brought out of a stone a flood of water pure,
And out of the hardest stone oil abundantly;
Right so out of our precious stone if thou be witty,
    Oil inconbustible and water thou shalt draw,
    And thereabout thou needest not at the coals to blow.

(Every line of this poem applies to the whole of the process although it may appear the instructions are specially for the work in hand. Keep this fact well in mind when experimenting, otherwise seeing certain colours and changes at any one point may mislead you. Besides the main colours of black, white and finally red, you may see green, yellow and a number of other colours come to the surface and soon disappear. This is in the nature of Antimony).

Do this with heat easy and measuring,
First with moist fire, and after with the dry,
The phlem with patience outdrawing,
And after that thy other natures wittily,
Dry up thine earth till it be thirsty;
    By calcining, else thou labourest all in vain,
    Then make it drink up its moisture again.

(This whole gate of separation has to do with distillation. The researcher is advised to study this gate well, intently and closely as so much depends on this part of the work. The matter will forever remain black while the wetness is in it. When the water is drawn off, different colours will arise, and with the return of the water, blackness will return; but study the gate of separation well, and you will be led to do the correct thing.)

Separation thus must thou often times make,
Thy matter dividing into parts two.

So that the simple from the gross thou take,
Till the earth remain below in colour blue.
That earth is fixed to abide all woe,
    The other part is spiritual and flying,
    But thou must turn them all into one thing.

The water wherewith thou must revive thy stone,
Look thou distill before thou work with it,
Often times by itself alone;
And by thy sight thou shalt well wit,
From feculent faeces when it is quit,
    For some men can with Saturn it multiply,
    And other substances which we defie.

(The last two sentences are put in just to mystify and mislead.)

Distill it therefore till be clean,
And thin like water as it should be,
As heaven in colour bright and shine,
Keeping both figure and ponderosity.
Therewith did Hermes moisten his tree.
    In his glass he made it to grow upright,
    With flowers discoloured beautiful to sight.

This water is like to the venomous Tyre,
Wherewith the mighty miracle is wrought,
For it is a poison most strong of ire,
A stronger poison none can be thought;
Oftentimes at the chemist it is sought,
    But no man shall be by it intoxicate,
    After the time it is into medicine elevate.

For then it is the miracle true,
It is of poisons most expulsive,
And in its workings does marvels show,
Preserving many from death to life,
Look thou mix it with no corrosives.
    But choose it pure and quick running,
    If thou thereby will have winning.

(All of which means nothing more than distil the liquid out of it, leaving the matter dry, before returning it. What follows explains that this must be done seven times.)

It is a marvellous thing in kind,
And without it nought can be done.
Therefore did Hermes call it his wind,
For it is uprising from sun and moon,
And maketh our stone to fly with it soon.
    Reviving the dead and giving life,
    To sun and moon, husband and wife.

Which if they were not by craft made quick,
And their fatness with water drawn out,
And so the thin dissevered from the thick,
Thou should never bring this work about.
If thou wilt speed therefore without doubt,
    Raise up thy birds out of their nest,
    And after bring them again to rest.

Water with water will accord and ascend,
And spirit with spirit, for they be of a kind,
Which after they be exalted make to descend;
So shalt thou unloose that which nature did blend.
Mercury essential turning into wind
    Without which natural and subtle separation,
    May never complete profitable generation.

Now to help thee in at this gate,
The last secret I will tell to thee;
Thy water must be seven times sublimate,
Else shall no kindly dissolution be,
Not putrefying shall thou not see.
    Like liquid pitch nor colours appearing,
    For lack of fire within thy glass working.

Therefore make fire thy glass within,
Which burneth the bodies more than fire
Elemental: If thou wilt win our secret

According to thy desire;
Then shall thy seed both rot and spire,
    By help of fire occasionate,
    That kindly after they may be separate.

Of separation the gate must thus be won,
That furthermore yet thou mayest proceed,
Toward the gate of secret conjunction,
Into the inner castle which will thee lead.
Do after my counsel therefore if thou wilt speed.
    With two strong locks this gate is shut,
    As consequently now thou must cut.

9. Consummation of the Hermetic Marriage

Twelve Gates (continued)

CONJUNCTION—*The Fourth Gate*

After the chapter of natural separation,
By which the elements of our stone dissevered be,
The chapter here followeth of secret conjunction:
Which repugnant natures joineth to perfect unity.
And so them kniteth that none from the other may flee.
> When they by fire shall be examinate,
> So if they be together surely conjugate.

And therefore philosophers giveth this definition,
Saying this conjunction is nought else,
But of dissevered qualities a copulation,
Or of principles a coequation, as others tell;
But some with mercury which the apothecary sell,
> Medleth bodies which cannot divide,
> Their matter, and therefore they step aside.

For until the time the soul be separate,
And cleansed from its original sin,
With the water, and purely spiritualizate,
Thy true conjunction may thou never begin.
Therefore first the soul from the body twin,
> Then of the corporal part and the spiritual,
> The soul shall cause conjunction perpetual.

(Take good care now that you do not begin to distil the matter until it is black and properly putrefied, which will not take place before 42 to 90 days.)

109

Of two conjunctions the philosophers do mention make;
Gross when the body with mercury is incrudate.
But let this pass, and to the second heed take,
Which is as I have said, after separation celebrate;
In which the parties be left, and so collegate,
    And so promoted unto perfect temperence,
    That never after may be among them repugnance.

This chapter I will conclude right soon, therefore
Gross conjunction charging you to make but one,
For seldom have strumpets children of them bore,
And so thou shalt never come by our stone,
Without you suffer the woman to lie alone.
    That after she has conceived of the man,
    The matrix of her be shut from all others then.

For such as addeth evermore crude to crude,
Opening their vessels and letting their matters cool,
The sperm conceived, they nourish not, but delude
themselves, and spilleth their work each deal.
Therefore if thou list to do well,
    Close up the matrix and nourish the seed,
    With heat continual and temperate, if thou wilt speed.

And when thy vessel has stood by months five,
And clouds and eclipses be passed each one,
Then light appearing, increase thy heat, then blive
Till white and shining in brightness be thy stone;
Then mayest thou open thy glass anon,
    And feed thy child which then is bore,
    With milk and meat, aye more and more.

And in two things all our intent doth hinge;
In moist and dry which be contrarious two;
In dry that it the moist to fixing bring,
In moist that it give liquefaction the earth unto,
That of them thus contemperate may go forth,
    A temperament not so thick as the body is,
    Neither so thin as the water is without miss.

Loosing and knitting together be principles two,
Of this hard science, and poles most principle:
How be it that other principles be many more,
As shining sanells which show I shall.
Proceed therefore unto another wall
> Of this strong castle of our wisdom,
> That inner at the fifth gate thou may come.

(The next gate given is "Putrefaction", but on no account must the student take it for granted that this is a fifth stage or process. These Gates are purposely written out of order to confuse and mislead. In fact putrefaction should have been put first in the order of working.)

PUTREFACTION—The Fifth Gate

Now beginneth the chapter of putrefaction,
Without which pole no seed can multiply.
Which must be done only by continual action,
Of heat in the body, moist not manually,
For bodies else may not be altered naturally.
> Since Christ do it witness, without the grain of wheat,
> Die in the ground, increase may thou not get.

And likewise without thy matter do putrefy,
It may in no wise truly be alterate,
Nor thine elements be divided kindly,
Nor thy conjunction of them kindly celebrate;
That thy labour therefore be not frustrate,
> The privity of putrefying well understand,
> Before ever thou take this work in hand.

And putrefaction may thus defined be,
After philosophers sayings, it is of bodies the slaying,
And in our compound a division of things three.
The killing of bodies unto corruption forth leading,
And after unto generation them abling.
> For things being earth without doubt,
> Be engendered of rotation of the heavens about.

111

And therefore as I have said before,
Thine elements comixt and wisely coequate,
Thou keep in temperate heat, eschewing evermore,
That they by violent heat be never incinerate,
To powder dry unprofitably rubyficate.
> But into black powder as a crow's bill,
> With heat of a bath, or else our dunghill.

To the time when nights be passed ninety.
In moist heat keep them from any thing.
Soon after my blackness thou shalt espy
That they draw fast to putrefying,
Which thou shalt after many colours bring,
> To perfect whiteness with patience easily,
> And so thy seed in his nature will multiply.

Make each the other to hug and kiss,
And like as children to play them up and down;
And when their skirts are filled like this, [with liquid]
Then let the woman to wash to bound,
Which often for faintness will fall in a swoon,
> And die at last with her children all,
> And go to purgatory to purge original.

(In the last verse in the chapter on "Solution", one is told, "Beware thy glass thou never open nor move", and here in this last verse, one is told: "Make each the other to hug and kiss, and play them up and down" to mix the liquid well into the compound. The experimenter will have to try both ways to find the true method. That is why more than one experiment must be started. We have already quoted Flamel as saying: "and no more labour is required, than that they should be every day turned, like a chicken on her eggs, that the chickens may be sooner hatched, and better, concerning which enough is said".)

When they be there, by little and little increase,
Their pains with heat, aye, more and more;
The fire from them let never cease.

112

And see thy furness be apt therefore,
Which wise men do call Athenor: [continually hot]
    Conserving heat required most temperately,
    By which the water doth kindly putrefy.

Of this principle speaketh sapient Guido,
And sayeth "By rotting dieth the compound corporal",
And then after Morien and others more,
Upriseth again regenerate, simple and spiritual;
And were not heat and moisture continual,
    Sperm in the womb might have none abiding,
    And so should there be no fruit providing.

Therefore at the beginning our stone thou take,
And bury each one with other within their grave,
Then equally a marriage betwixt them make;
To lie together six weeks let them have,
Their seed conceived kindly to nourish and save,
    From the ground of their grave not rising that while,
    Which secret point doth many a one beguile.

(The last four lines may give the answer to the problem of whether
or not to move the flask. We are told, "six weeks let them have".)

This time of conception, with easy heat abide,
That blackness showing shall tell thee when they die;
For they together liquid pitch that tide,
Shall swell and bubble, settle and putrefy;
Shining colours therein shalt thou espy:
    Like to the rainbow, marvellous unto sight,
    The water then beginneth to dry upright.

For in moist bodies, heat nourishing temperate,
Engendereth blackness first of all, which is
Of kindly commixtion be the token assignate;
And of true putrefying; remember this.
For then to alter perfectly thou may not miss.
    And thus by the gate of blackness thou must come in;
    To light of paradise in whiteness if thou wilt win.

For first the sun in his uprising obscurate,
Shall be, and pass the waters of Noah's flood,
On earth; which were a hundred continuate,
And fifty, ere away all this water yode. [went]
Right so our waters as wise men understood,
> Shall pass, that thou with David may say,
> Abierunt in sicco flumina: bare this away.

(Each one of the masters in alchemy had his own idea of how long it took to bring the processes to perfection; for each had to discover the secret for himself. The present author thinks it takes three months to the black and white, and then five months to the red.)

And that thou may rather to putrefaction win,
This example take thou to thee for a true conclusion
For all the secret of putrefaction lieth therein:
The heart of oak that hath of water continual infusion,
will not soon putrefy, I tell thee without delusion:
> For though it in water lie a hundred years or more,
> Yet should thou find it sound as ever it was before.

But if thou keep it sometimes wet, and sometime dry,
As thou mayest see in timber by usual experiment,
By process of time that oak shall utterly putrefy.
And so likewise according to our intent,
Sometimes our tree must with the sun be brent:
> And then with water soon after must we it cool,
> That by this means shalt rotting bring it well.

For now in wet, and now again in dry,
Now in great heat and now again in cold
To be, shall cause it soon for to putrefy:
And so shalt thou bring to rotting thy gold,
Treat thy bodies therefore as I have thee told:
> And in thy putrefying with heat be not so swift,
> Lest in the ashes thou seek after thy thrift.

(All this and what follows after having been told not to move or open the glass! How is this to be done? Maybe it would be wise to

114

start the first process in a distilling retort glass, then one may just tip
the retort so that the water distils into the receiver.)

Therefore the water out of the earth thou draw,
And make the soul therewith to ascend,
Then down again into the earth it throw,
That they offtimes so ascend and descend,
From violent heat and sudden cold defend
    Thy glass, and make thy fire so temperate,
    That by the sides thy water be never vitrified.

Now in this chapter I have thee taught,
How thou the bodies must putrefy;
And so to guide thee thou be not caught,
And put in durance, loss, and villanie,
My doctrine therefore remember wittily,
    And pass towards the sixth gate,
    For this the fifth is triumpthate.

CONGEALATION—The Sixth Gate

Of congealation, I need not much to write,
But what it is now, I will first declare,
It is of soft things of colour white, induration.
And of spirits which slaying are, confixation.
How to congeal, thee needeth not much to care;
    For elements will knit together soon,
    If that putrefaction be kindly done.

The earthly grossness therefore first mortified,
In moistness, blackness engendered is:
This principle may not be denied,
For natural philosophers so sayeth, I wis,
Which had, of whiteness thou may not miss.
    And into whiteness if thou congeal it once,
    Thou hast a stone most precious of all stones.

And by the dry like as the moist did putrefy.
Which caused in colours blackness to appear,
Right so, the moist congealed by the dry,

115

Engendereth whiteness shining with might most clear,
And dryness proceedeth as whiteness the matter;
  Like as in blackness, moistness doth him show,
  By colours variant aye new and new.

(The matter, whatever its stage, will always remain black until
dried out, for only when the matter is dry will vapour arise.)

The cause of all this is heat most temperate.
Working and moving the matter continually;
And thereby also the matter is alterate,
Both inward and outward substantially,
And not as doth fools to sight sophistically.
  But every part all fire to endure,
  Fluxibly fix and stable in tincture.

And physick determineth of each digestion,
First done in the stomach in which is dryness,
Causing whiteness without question,
Like as the second digestion causeth redness,
Complete in the matter by heat and temperateness;
  And so our stone by dryness and by heat,
  Digested is to white and red complete.

But here thou must another secret know,
How the philosopher's child in the air is born:
Busy thee not too fast at the coal to blow,
And take that neither for mock not scorn,
But trust me truly else thy work is all forlorn,
  Without thine earth with water revived be,
  Our true congealing shalt thou never see.

A soul betwixt heaven and earth being;
Arising from the earth as air with water pure.
And causing life in every living thing,
Incessant running upon our aforesaid nature,
Enforcing to better them with all his cure;
  Which air is the fire of our philosophy,
  Named now oil, now water mistily.

116

And by this means, air, oil, or water we call,
Our fire, our ointment, our spirit, and our stone,
In which we ground, in one thing, our wisdoms all,
Goeth neither out nor in alone,
Never the flier but the water anon:
    First it outleadeth, and after bringeth it in,
    As water with water, which will not lightly twin.

And truly this is the cause principal,
Why philosophers charge us to be patient,
Till time the water were dried to powder all,
With nourishing heat continual but not violent;
For qualities be contrarious of every element,
    Till after black in white be made a union.
    And then forever congealed without division.

And furthermore the preparation of this conversion,
From thing to thing, from one state to another,
Is done only by kindly and discreet operation,
Of nature, as is of sperm-within the mother:
For sperm and heat be as sister and brother,
    Which be converted by themselves as nature can,
    By action and passion, at last to perfect man.

In the time of this seed process natural,
While that sperm conceived is growing,
The substance is nourished with his own menstrual,
Which water only out of the earth did bring;
Whose colour is green in the first showing;
    And for that time the sun hideth his light,
    Taking his course through the North by night.

The said menstrue is (I say to thee in councel),
The blood of our green lion and not of vitriol;
Dame venus can the truth of this thee tell,
At the beginning, to councel if thou her call,
This secret is hid by philosophers great and small,
    Which blood is drawn out of the said lion,
    For lack of heat had not perfect digestion.

117

(This last verse reveals the secret that one should never use copper or venus in alchemical work: copper gives out a green colour but spoils the work.)

But this blood, our secret menstrual,
Wherewith our sperm is nourished temperately,
When it is turned into the faeces corporal,
And becomes perfectly white and very dry,
Congealed and fixed into his own body,
  Then bursting blood to the sight it may well seem,
  Of this work named the milk white diadem.

Understand now that our fiery water thus actuate,
Is called our menstrual water, wherein
Our earth is lost and naturally calcinate,
By congealation that they may never twin;
Yet to congeal more water thou may not blin, [hesitate]
  Into three parts of the earth congealed and no more,
  With the fourth part of the actuate water, said before.

Unto that substance therefore so congealate,
The fourth part put of water crystalline,
And make them then together to be dispensate,
By congealation into a minor metalline:
Which like a new slipped sword then will shine,
  After the blackness which first will show,
  The fourth part give it of water new.

When thou has made seven times imbibition,
Again thou must turn thy wheel,
And putrefy all that matter without addition;
First blackness abiding if thou wilt do well,
Then into whiteness congeal it up each deal.
  And by redness into the south descend,
  Then hast thou brought thy base to an end.

Thus is thy water then divided in parts two.
With the first part the bodies to putreficate,
And to thine imbibitions the second part must go,

With which the matter is afterwards denigrate,
And soon upon it by easy decoction albificate.
  Then it is named by philosophers our stary stone,
  Bring that to redness, then is the six gate won.

(It will soon be discovered that every instruction for each stage is reiterated and spread throughout the whole of the work of producing the Philosophers' Stone; each bit of information might equally well apply to the black state, the white, or the red. We are warned not to move the flask or open it, yet we are to distil the contents, imbibe it with the water we extract, and so on. Read and re-read the different treatises to be found in this book, and by trial and error things will begin to finally clarify. The time required to complete the work is the great bugbear; remember it was not the adepts' intention to expose the whole secret to every dilettante, so patience and perseverence are required above all things.)

10.   The Use of the Stone

CIBATION—The Seventh Gate

Now of cibation I turn my pen to write,
Since it must here the seventh place occupy.
But in a few words it will be expedite,
Take intent thereto, and understand me wittily,
Cibation is called a feeding of our matter dry,
  With milk and meat, which moderately they do,
  Till it be brought the third order unto.

But first give it not so much that thou it glut,
Beware of the dropsy, and of Noah's flood;
By little and little therefore to it put,
Of meat and drink as seemeth to do it good,
That watery humours not overgrow the blood:
  The drink therefore let it be measured so.
  That kindly appetite thou never quench therefro.

For if it drink too much, then must it have
A vomit, else will it be sick too long,
From the dropsy therefore thy womb thou save,
And from the flux, else will it be wrong;
Which rather let it thirst for drink awhile.
  Than thou should give it overmuch at once,
  Which must in youth be dieted for the nonce.

And if thou diet it as nature doth require,
Moderately until it be grown up to age,
From cold it keeping and nourishing with moist fire;

121

Then shall it grow and wax full of courage,
And do thee both pleasure and advantage.
　　For it shall make dark bodies whole and bright,
　　Cleansing their leprosies with all his might.

Three times thus must thou turn about thy wheel,
About keeping the rule of the said cibation;
And then as soon as it the fire doth feel,
Like wax it will be ready unto liquidation:
This chapter needeth not longer protraction.
　　For I have told thee the dietry most convenient.
　　After thine elements be made equipolent.

And also how thou to whiteness shall bring thy gold,
Most like in figure to the lenies of an Hawthorn tree,
Called magnesia afore as I have told.
And our white sulphur without combustability.
Which from the fire away will never flee.
　　And thus the seventh gate as thou desired.
　　In the uprising of the sun is conquered.

(Presented in medieval language and poetry, it is not easy to follow the advice given, especially when it is offered in a manner designed to cast doubts on every move one makes. It will always be necessary to re-read and study the other treatises presented in this book by way of cross-reference to confirm one's conclusions in each case.)

SUBLIMATION—*The Eighth Gate*

In subliming first beware of one thing;
That thou sublime not to the top of thy vessel,
For without violence thou shalt it not down bring,
Again, but there it will abide and dwell;
So it rejoiceth with refrigeration I thee tell.
　　Keep it therefore with temperate heat adown,
　　Full forty days, till it wax black abowen. [above]

For then the soul beginneth for to come out,
From his own veins: for all that subtle is,

122

Will with the spirits ascend withouten doubt:
Bear in thy mind therefore and think on this,
How here eclipsed have been thy bodies.
> As they do putrefy subliming more and more.
> Into the water till they be all bore.

And thus their venom when they have spouted out,
Into the water, then black it doth appear,
And become spiritual every deal without doubt,
Subliming easily according to our manner,
Into the water which doth him bear.
> For into the air our child thus be bore. [born]
> Of the water again as I said before.

(Sublimation can refer to any process in alchemy. It means the rarefying of the liquid in the glass, which must be kept closed, or in a retort receiver, from which the liquid is returned. When the water is at length withdrawn, the heat still continues to be applied, for then "The Alchemist's child is born", and a fine white vapour arises which is the alchemists' mercury, so much sought after.)

But when these to sublimation continual,
Be laboured so with heat both moist and temperate,
That all is white and purely made spiritual,
Then heaven upon earth must be reiterate,
Until the soul with the body be reincorporate.
> That earth will become all that before was heaven,
> Which will be done in sublimations seven.

And sublimation we make for causes three;
The first cause is to make the body spiritual,
The second that the spirit may corporal be,
And become fixed with it and substantial;
The third cause is that from his filth original,
> He may be cleansed, and his fatness suphurious,
> Be diminished in him which is infectious.

Then when they thus together purified be,
They will sublime up whiter than snow,

That sight will greatly comfort thee,
For then anon perfectly thou shalt know,
Thy spirits shall be adown I trow.
　　Then this gate to thee shall be unlocked,
　　For out of this gate many a one be shut out and mocked.

FERMENTATION—The Ninth Gate

That point I will disclose to thee,
Look how thou didst with thy imperfect body,
And do so with thy perfect body in every degree,
That is to say, first thou them putrefy
Her primary qualities destroying utterly:
　　For this is wholly to our intent,
　　That first thou alter before thou ferment.

To thy compound make ferment the forth part,
Which ferments be only of sun and moon.
If thou therefore be master of this art,
Thy fermentation let this be done,
Fix water and earth together soon:
　　And when the medicine as wax do flow,
　　Then upon the amalgam look thou it throw.

And when all that together is mixed,
Above thy glass well closed make thy fire,
And so continue till all be fixed,
And well fermented to thy desire,
Then make projection after thy pleasure,
　　For that is medicine then each deal perfect.
　　Thus must you ferment both red and white.

For like as flour of wheat made into paste,
Requireth ferment which leaven we call,
Of bread that it may have the kindly taste,
And become food to man and woman most cordial,
Right so thy medicine ferment thou shall
　　That it may taste with the ferment pure;
　　And all essays evermore endure.

124

The Use of the Stone

And understand that there be ferments three,
Two be of the bodies in nature clean,
Which must be altered as I have told thee,
The third most secret of which I mean,
Is the first earth to his own water green.
>> And therefore when the lion doth thirst,
>> Make him drink till his belly burst.

(This needs explaining. "Ferments three" are the antimony, iron
and gold or silver. The liquid catalyst on antimony will make it
green first of all, the iron will turn it red and black. These two metals
must first be properly compounded. Therefore for these two to be
properly mixed we have to give the compound enough drink "to
make its atoms dissolve"; or in the words of the poet, "till his belly
burst".)

But fermentation true as I thee tell,
Is of the soul with the bodies incorporation.
Restoring to it the kindly smell.
With taste and colour by natural confection,
Of things dissevered; a true reintegration.
>> Whereby the body of the spirit taketh impression,
>> That either of the other may have ingression.

For like as the bodies in their compaction corporal
May not show out their qualities effectually,
Until the time they become spiritual;
No more may spirits abide with the bodies steadfastly,
But with them be fixed proportionably;
>> For then the body teacheth the spirit to suffer fire,
>> And the spirit the body to endure to thy desire.

Therefore thy gold with gold thou must ferment;
With his own water cleansed, thine earth, I mean.
Or else to say but element with element;
The spirits of life only going between,
For like as an adament as thou hast seen,
>> Yearn to him draw, so doth our earth by kind,
>> Draw down to him his soul borne up by the wind.

With wind therefore thy soul lead out and in,
Mix gold with gold, that is to say,
Make elements with elements together run,
To time all fire they suffer may,
For earth is also ferment with a nay:
> To water, and water the earth unto
> Our fermentation in this wise must we go.

Earth is gold, and so is the soul also,
Not common gold, but ours thus elementate;
And yet the sun thereto must go,
That by our wheel it may be alterate.
For so to ferment it must be preparate
> That it profoundly may joined be,
> With other natures as I said to thee.

And whatsoever I have here said of gold,
The same of silver, I will thou understand,
That thou them putrefy and alter as I have told:
Ere thou thy medicine to ferment take in hand:
Forsooth, I could never him find in all the land,
> Which on this wise to ferment could me teach,
> Without error, by practice or by speech.

Thus with thy base after my doctrine preparate,
Which is our calx, this must be done.
For when our bodies be so calcinate,
Then water to oil dissolve them soon;
Make therefore oil of sun or moon.
> Which is a ferment most fragrant for to smell,
> And so the ninth gate is conquered of this well.

(This last verse speaks regarding an oil, most redolent, which reveals and is another process and which makes the medicine that cures all the diseases of man, the elixir of life.)

EXALTATION—The Tenth Gate

Proceed we now to the chapter of exaltation,
Of which truly thou must have knowledge pure;

126

Full little it is different from sublimation:
If thou conceive it right I thee ensure.
Hereto accordeth the holy scripture.
> Christ saying thus; if I exalted be,
> Then I shall draw all things to me.

(The third line of this verse states that exaltation is nothing else but sublimation, so this gate is altogether superfluous.)

If thou therefore thy bodies will exaltate,
First with the spirits of life thou them augment,
Till time thy earth be well subtilate,
By natural rectifying of each element,
Him exalting up into the firmament,
> Then much more precious shall they be than gold,
> Because they of the quintessence do hold.

For when the cold has overcome the heat,
Then into water the air shall turned be,
And so two contraries together shall meet,
Till either with other right well agree;
So into air thy water as I tell thee,
> When heat of cold has got dominion,
> Shall be converted by craft of circulation.

And of the fire, then air have thou shall,
By loosing, putrefying, and subliming;
And fire thou hast of the earth material,
Thy elements by craft thus dissevering,
Most specially the earth well calcining,
> And when they be each one made pure,
> Then do they hold all of the fifth nature.

In this wise therefore make them to circulate,
Each into other exalting by and by,
And in one glass do all this surely congealate,
Not with thy hands but as I teach thee naturally.
Fire into water then turn first hardily,
> For fire is in air, which is in water existent,
> And this conversion accordeth to our intent.

Then furthermore turn on thy wheel,
That into earth thy air converted be,
Which will be done also right well;
For air is in water being in earth trust me,
Then water into fire contrarious in this quality,
    Soon turn thou may, for water in earth is,
    Which is in fire conversion, true is this.

Thy wheel is now well nigh turned about;
Into air turn earth, which is the proper nest,
Of other elements there is no doubt,
For earth in fire is, which in air taketh rest,
This circulation thou must begin in the west.
    Then forth into the south until they exalted be,
    Proceed duly in the figure I have taught thee.

In which process thou mayest clearly see.
From an extreme how to another thou may not go;
But by a mean, since they in quality contrarious be;
And reason will show, forsooth, that it is so.
As heat into cold with other contraries more:
    Without their means, as moist to heat and cold.
    Examples sufficient, before this have I told.

Thus have I taught thee how to make,
Of all thy elements a perfect circulation.
And at thy figure example for to take;
How thou shalt make this aforesaid exaltation,
And of thy elements a true graduation.
    Till it be brought to a quite right temperate,
    And then thou hast conquered the tenth gate.

MULTIPLICATION—*The Eleventh Gate*

Multiplication now to declare I proceed,
Which is by philosophers in this wise defined.
Augmentation it is of that elixir indeed,
In goodness, in quantity, both for white and red.
Multiplication is therefore as they have said,
    That thing that doth augment the medicine in each degree.
    In colour, in odour, in virtue, and also in quantity.

And why thou may thy medicine multiply,
Infinitely, the cause forsooth is this;
For it is a fire which teigned will never die;
Dwelling with thee as fire doth in houses,
Of which one spark may make more fires, I wis;
>As musk in pigments, and other spices more.
>In virtue multiplyeth and our medicine right so.

So he is rich, the which fire hath less or more,
Because he may so greatly multiply;
And right so rich is he which any part hath in store,
Of our elixirs which be augmentable infinitely;
One way if thou dissolve our powders dry,
>And oft times of them make congealation,
>Of it in goodness thou maketh then augmentation.

The second way both in goodness and in quantity,
It multiplyeth by reiterate fermentation,
As in that chapter I showed plainly unto thee,
By divers manner of natural operation,
And also in the chapter of our cibation,
>Where thou may know how thou shalt multiply,
>Thy medicine with mercury infinitely.

(For more details of Multiplication, see Artephius, *The Secret Book*, paragraphs 44, 45 and 46 onwards.)

But if thou wilt loose and also ferment,
Both more in quantity and better will it be;
And in such wise thou may that so augment,
That in thy glass it will grow like a tree,
The Tree of Hermes named, seemly to see,
>Of which one pepin a thousand will multiply,
>If thou can make thy projection wittily.

And like as saffron when it is pulverisate,
By little and little if it in liquor be
Tempered, and then with much more liquor dilate,

Tingeth much of liquor in quantity,
Than being whole in his own gross nature: so shalt thou
    That our elixirs the more they be made thin,
    The further in tincture so softly will run.

Keep in thy fire therefore both evening and morrow,
From house to house, that thou need not to run,
Among thy neighbours, thy fire to fetch or borrow;
The more thou keepest, the more good shalt thou win,
Multiplying more and more thy glass within,
    By feeding with mercury to thy life's end,
    So shalt thou have more than thou needest to spend.

This matter is plain, I will say no more.
Right now thereof, let reason thee guide,
Be never the bolder to sin therefore,
But serve thy God the better at each tide:
And whilst thou shalt in this life abide.
    Bear this in mind, forget not I thee pray.
    As thou shalt appear before thy God one day.

His own great gifts therefore and His treasure
Dispose thou virtuously helping the poor at need,
That in this world to thee thou may procure
Mercy and grace with heavenly bliss to mede.
And pray devoutly to God that he thee lead.
    In this eleventh Gate He will thee best.
    Soon after then thou shalt end thy quest.

PROJECTION—The Twelfth Gate

In projection it shall be proved if our practice be profitable,
Of which it behoveth me the secrets here to move,
Therefore if thy tincture be sure and not variable,
By a little of this medicine thus shall thou prove,
With metal or mercury as pitch it will cleve,
    And tinct in projection all fires to abide,
    And soon it will enter and spread full wide.

But many through ignorance doth mar what they made,
When on metals uncleaned projection they make
For because of corruption their tincture must fade,
Which they would not away first from bodies take,
Which after projection be brittle, blue and black:
     That thy tincture therefore may evermore last.
     Upon ferment thy medicine look thou first cast.

Then brittle will thy ferment as any glass be,
Upon bodies cleaned and made very pure,
Cast thy brittle substance and soon thou shalt see,
That they shall be curiously coloured with tincture,
Which at all essays for ever shall endure.
     But at the psalmist and psalter example thou take,
     Profitable projection perfectly to make.

On fundamenta cast first this psalme nunc dimittis;
Upon verba mea then cast fundamenta blive, [quickly]
Then verba mea upon diligram, conceive me with thy wits,
And diligram on attende, if thou wish to thrive;
Thus make thou projection three, four or five.
     Till the tincture of thy medicine begin to decrease,
     Then it is time for projection to cease.

By this misty talking I mean nothing else,
But that thou must cast first the less on the more,
Increasing ever the number as wise men thee tells;
And keep thou this secret to thyself in store,
Be covertous of cunning, it is no burden sore:
     For he that joineth not the elixirs with bodies made clean,
     He knows not surely what projection doth mean.

Ten if thou multiply first into ten,
One hundred that number will make assuredly;
If one hundred into a hundred be multiplied then,
Then thousand is the number count it wittily,
Then into much more than ten thousand multiply:
     That is a thousand thousand, which multiplieth I wis,
     Into as much more as a hundred million is.

131

That hundred millions be multiplied likewise,
Into ten thousand millions, that is to say.
Maketh so great a number I wot not what it is,
Thy number in projection thus multiply always;
Now child of thy courtesy for me thou pray.
     Since that I have told thee our secrets both all and some.
     To which I beseech God by Grace thou may come.

Now thou hast conquered the twelve Gates.
And all the castle thou holdest at will,
Keep thy secrets in store unto thy self,
And the commandments of God look thou fulfill,
In fire continue to keep thy glass still.
     And multiply thy medicine aye more and more,
     For wise men did say that store is no sore.

END OF THE TWELVE GATES

11. Sulphur and Salt

To recapitulate, the interested student should now possess the whole picture of the art of alchemy, both in theory and in practice. Indeed he should have gained enough knowledge of the subject to enable him to commence research by practical experiment. Few of those who studied the art from books in the past ever learned much: their reading could give them no idea even of the materials to practise upon. The few books published in later years by modern scientists are mainly fragmentary and a rehash from older treatises, padded with comment which, at best, is meaningless instruction, only serving to leave the reader more perplexed. Thus they have buried the whole art deeper still.

The student is recommended to follow Pontanus's advice, remembering what he said regarding Artephius and his *Secret Book*, it being the only one among thousands that he found to be true, clearly written, frank, and useful. Therefore the researcher should return again and again to this *Secret Book* for confirmation, studying it closely and noting carefully what is laid down therein.

To repeat what has been already said, the main reason for failure in finding the true road to success has been ignorance of the true mercury, which is nothing else than the metallic vapour of Antimony purified by iron, with which everything is done, and without which nothing will be achieved. Although it is well known to the modern metallurgist that ordinary mercury or quicksilver (or argent vive, as the alchemists called it) will mix with most metals, and reduce them to a liquid condition even at room temperature, many experimenters of old failed, as they never imagined that anything else could take its place. Thus they never gave up experimenting with this metal. But mercury will separate from any metal with which it has been amalgamated if it is heated. As soon as a correct heat is applied, it separates and as the alchemist's work was to produce a fixed metal that would not do this, ordinary mercury was not the answer.

An important treatise on Antimony entitled *The Triumphal Chariot of Antimony*, by Basilius Valentinus, gives us this valuable hint. The treatise was written from a medicinal angle, by a monk: remember, the "Elixir of Life" is another name for the "Philosophers' Stone".

"Therefore one should not think any labour too great, which is likely to advance his knowledge of antimony . . . one should in the first place become acquainted with the manner of its solution, so as to proceed in the right way, without entering into devious paths. Secondly he should learn how to regulate the fire, so that it be neither too fierce or too feeble. Fire is the root of the whole matter. By means of the fire, the vital spirits are extracted and dissolved for the purposes of the operation. But care must be taken not to destroy the spirit by means of too much fire."

It should always be remembered that the Philosophers' Stone must be produced in a natural manner, which to the adepts meant long digestion in a heat not much more than blood heat, which they term cooking. Later in a dry stage they used a greater heat, which they called roasting, never more than the heat required for the roasting of food. The red powder apparently could stand the greatest heat, more than the white stage, but a heat below the melting point of gold. The heat required to melt metals in a furnace would "kill" them, according to the true alchemists. The whole business must be brought about naturally, and that meant slowly working up to the highest temperature during which period the experimenter could watch the matter in the glass changing colour and condition. The stages followed the pattern, first black, then white, next citrine, and finally blood red, and in that order only. But in between these colours, all the colours of the rainbow were generated. These various colours were often referred to as the "peacock's tail". If the main colours were out of order then this was a warning of error in the experiment.

Also too much accumulated heat often burst the vessel during the drying and rarefying of the liquid in the glass. This liquid was the catalyst, the "secret fire" spoken of earlier, the mercury, which vaporised, arose from the compound, and was cooled in the neck of the flask, before condensing again into a liquid, and falling back into the bottom of the flask. If when the long neck of the flask was not some degrees cooler than the compound below, the vapour would expand too rapidly and explode the vessel.

The alchemists believed that when creation started, seed was granted to everything in creation, and metals were no exception; for to the adepts, metals are also living things. We all know where the seed of animals and vegetables are to be found, but the great secret of alchemy is to know that the seed of metals is to be found in or by the aid of their vapour, and by this they are able to produce their kind *ad infinitum* as with all other created things. Artephius has claimed "that the whole of this secret is antimony and a mercurial sublimate". This sublimate of antimony is a white vapour. But do not think that even Artephius has quite casually given the whole secret away to everyone who tries his hand at making gold: it must be laboured for.

True, the adepts have claimed that the work is "child's play and woman's work", and so it is, but only to those who have the "know-how", and this has eluded countless clever minds for hundreds of years. The very simplicity of the work may have been the cause, for nature is simple in all her works. The unveiling of a secret of such a tremendous importance could be a blessing to mankind but it could also be a curse, and the masters of the art appreciated this fact in a world of selfishness, greed and brutality, and therefore they used all their ingenuity to hide the knowledge, and those who found it did likewise.

Here follow extracts concerning sulphur, mercury and the secret fire from a comparatively modern publication entitled *Bacstrom's Alchemical Anthology* published by Watkins in 1960 and edited by J. W. Hamilton-Jones.

WHAT IS SULPHUR

"The invisible tinging spirit is the pure fire of Gold . . . The father of the stone is Sol. [Gold is sulphur]

"As gold is the most perfect of all metals, so gold contains the tincture of redness. Silver is a tincture of perfect whiteness.

"He who knows how to make a tinging venom from gold or its shadow that is Luna [i.e. common silver] obtains our stone. [Gold or silver is mixed with the prepared mercury]

135

"He who knows not how to extract the soul from the body of gold, and return it to the body, wholly deviates from the right path.

"Whosoever desires to enjoy the secret of the 'Golden Fleece', let him know that our gold making powder [which we call our stone] is only gold digested into the highest degree of purity and subtile fixity, whereto it may be brought, by nature and a discreet artist; which gold thus essensified, is called our gold [and is no more vulgar] and is the period of the perfection of nature, and of art. Let gold therefore be the one true sole principle of gold making. This doth in our work supply the place of the male, and therefore it is joined to our white and more crude gold [the regulus of antimony and mars]. Sulphur doth, in this work, supply the place of the male. [Observe that Sol is here called sulphur.]

"Nature is to be amended by its own nature, that is gold or silver are to be exalted in our water. [Luna is antimony and Mars reduced to water, which is also known as mercury.]

"Gold will yield fruit and seed, in which it multiplies itself, by the industry of the skilful artist, who knows how to exalt nature. The body which yields the seed is gold; Our silver [the regulus of antimony and mars], is that which receives the seed of the gold. This Luna is the garden in which the noble scion is planted.

"Seek not the principles of gold anywhere else; for in gold is the seed of gold: though being shut up it retires in deed and is to be sought by us with tedious labour.

"Two metals are more pure than the rest, namely gold and silver without which the work cannot be begun or finished; because in them is the purest substance of sulphur, perfectly purified by the ingenuity of nature.

"Sol, which is our sulphur, is reduced into mercury by mercury. [Mercury is the regulus of antimony and iron.]

"Therefore, my son observe that the red philosophical sulphur is in the gold . . . all philosophers do witness that the red sulphur is gold.

"If you wish to obtain the greatest secret you must endeavour not only to purify the vulgar gold, but also to tinge it so that it may become seven times more red. To make Sol more perfect than it is naturally, is not in the power of nature, but this may and must be accomplished by an intelligent artist if he wishes to obtain the jewel of knowledge.

136

WHAT IS "OUR MERCURY"

"A crude immature and coagulated mercury vive, not yet fixed, is the destroyer of the perfect bodies [i.e. gold and silver], for truly it destroys them, incrudates and softens them, and renders them fit for our work. It is the only and greatest secret in the whole art. The sign of its right preparation is a beautiful whiteness, like the purest silver, a heavenly brightness, and a wonderful glittering on the face of its fractures when broken, like the polish of a bright sword . . . [this is a description of the raw metal]. The mercury of the philosophers [regulus of antimony and mars], is not found in the earth, but must be prepared by art, by joining the sulphur [of mars] to the mercury [of antimony]. He never shows himself openly in his naked form. He is put under a disguise by nature [it is found in the form of a sulphuret]. We say sulphur and mercury are the minera of our Venus in a crude state [i.e. common sulphur and antimony]; and this mercury has the power to unlock, kill and revive the metals, which power it has received from the acid sulphur of its own Nature. [Venus is here added to cause a problem. Some have called it useless and others say a little is necessary.]

"Antimony is a mineral participating of saturnine parts and has in all respects the nature thereof. This saturnine antimony agrees with gold and contains in itself argentum vivum, in which no metal is swallowed up except gold; and gold is truly swallowed up by this antimonial argent vive . . . for this water is friendly and agrees with the metals, whitening gold, because it contains in itself white or pure argent vive.

"Let the two heroes saturn [antimony] and mars [iron] fight together. Though the former is peaceably inclined, let them have three or four violent assaults [viz. by the addition of nitre in the glass when making the regulus]. After this they will be reconciled and as a token thereof they will erect a glorious banner resembling a star.

"All the metals have their rise from water, the root of all metals. Therefore they are reduced into water, as ice by heat is reduced into water—because it hath been water before. . . . It [our water] disposeth the bodies [of gold and silver] readily. It is father and mother; it openeth and shutteth, and reduceth metals into what they were in the

137

beginning. It disposeth the bodies and coagulates itself along with them. The spirit [our secret fire] is carried upon the water [i.e. is added to it]; that is, the power of the spirit is seen to operate there, which is done when [or after] the body is put into the water [i.e. The secret fire must not be added till after you have made Rebis] . . . one of the greatest secrets is to free this stone or mercury vive from its natural bonds . . . that is to reduce and dissolve it into its primordial water [the natural crude sulphur must be separated from it, and the sulphur of mars substituted] for unless this is done, all will prove lost labour. . . .

"Let him who by divine assistance obtaineth this blessed water render thanks to God, for he hath the key in his hands wherewith he may open the fast locks of all metallic chests.

WHAT IS "OUR SECRET FIRE"

"Our philosophical mercurial water [secret fire] is the key whereby all coagulated, fixed and unfixed metallic and mineral bodies are radically and physically dissolved and reduced into their first principles. This mercurial water has been kept very secret by all the philosophers, as the secret of the whole art.

"When this spirit [mercury] has been sublimed [converted into sublimate] it is called, the water which washes and cleanses itself; because [in the work] it ascends with its most subtile essence and leaves its corrupting particles behind. This ascension has been called distillation, washing, and sublimation.

"Our whole secret and work is made with our water, and from it and by it we obtain all that we require. It dissolves the body, not by a common solution as the ignorant think, who [the word 'who' is a stumbling block, leave it out] look for a clear water like that of rain, but by a true philosophical solution, so that the body is converted into an unctuous and viscous water [Azoth], out of which the metals were originally formed.

"Our moist fire, by dissolving and subliming that which is pure and white, casts forth or rejects its faeces or filth, like a voluntary vomit . . . the pure and white substance ascends upwards, and the impure and earthy remains fixed in the bottom . . . this must be taken away and removed because it is of no value, taking only the middle white substance rejecting the foeculeus earth which remains

138

below [also any light flowers which rise into the neck of the subliming vessel].

"The clear, white, pure and clean matter [in place of the word 'matter' read 'water'] is wholly and only to be taken and made use of. This sublimation is without doubt, the key of the whole work . . . in this whiteness [sublimation] the antimonial and mercurial soul is by natural compact infused into and joined with the spirits of Sol or Luna . . . in this whiteness is the soul infused into the body. [This is the priest that joins the male and female into an indissoluble union.]

"I will tell thee, and that faithfully, what kind of water this is, it is the water of Salt Peter which is known as mercury. [It is like Salt Peter, a white salt known to be mercurial.] Whosoever has once made our water, nothing remains to be done but to cast in a clean body in a just quantity, shut the vessel and so let it stand till the compliment of the work.

"Our sulphur [Sol] when it is joined with its water [our luna] or mercury doth little by little consume and drink up the same by the help of the fire.

"In our work, we must attend to the weight of the sulphur in the mercury. And since, as I have told, the element of fire does not predominate in mercury, in its crude state which is the very thing which digests the matter, it is necessary to know how much more subtle the element of fire is than the other elements [viz. of our compound] and what proportion of it [by weight] is necessary to conquer them."

(Distilled vinegar, often mentioned in alchemical literature, is not the vinegar of the philosophers. Their most sharp vinegar is the secret fire, which extracts the essence from the regulus of antimony and mars and forms azoth, which is again "our mercury".)

WHAT IS "REBIS" (Two things)

"The error in this work is chiefly attributed to the ignorance of the true fire, which is one of the moving principles that transmutes the whole matter into the true philosophers' stone. . . . In a short time, that fire without any laying on of hands will complete the whole work. . . . And by means of this our fire the medicine will be multiplied—if joined with the crude matter—not only in quantity,

139

but also in quality or virtue. Therefore seek out this fire with all thy industry for having once found it thou shalt accomplish thy desire, because it performs the whole work, and is the true key of all the philosophers, which they have never yet revealed.

"The whole art is comprehended in . . . Sol or Luna [gold or silver] and mercury. . . . In two of these is found the sulphur white and red. [The Philosophers' Stone is a white or red powder.] . . . The tinging rays . . . but the stone of mercury unites and binds them both. [The stone of mercury is the secret fire.]

"We have three conjunctions, all of which must be known by him who intends to complete the mastery. The first is gross; it is the amalgamation by fusion of the regulus of antimony and mars, which compound is called "Rebis", that is two things. Res Rebis est una confecta. In this mixture there are two natures, the one more active, and the other more passive.

"The beginning of this art is only one thing [Rebis] composed of two substances. . . . The one is the red fixed servant and the other is the wife. [Later] One is Sol, which is the seed, and the other is the mother. One is Sulphur, and the other is mercury [antimony and mars].

"As gold is the most perfect of all the metals, so gold contains the tincture of redness—silver a white tincture, tinging with perfect whiteness. With these bodies the mercury is mixed [with either of them], and is fixed [by its digestion afterwards with the secret fire].

"The invisible tinging spirit is the pure fire of Gold. This is concealed and caught in the centre of the coagulated salt [our mercury].

"The universal medicine which cures all human and metallic diseases is concealed in gold and its magnet [the regulus of antimony and mars], the Chalibs of Sendivogius.

"The true matter has been named by various appellations, so in truth it is one thing, Rebis, the philosophers mercury. [It is called Hermaphrodite when the regulus of antimony and mars is animated with Sol.]

"First take thy body which is gold and thy water [the regulus of antimony and mars] which is mercury—the one [gold] ready made by nature to hand, and the other thou must prepare. . . . Mix these together in due proportion.

"Make the marriage between the red man and his white wife and thou shalt have the master.

140

TEMPERATURE, FURNACE, AND GLASS

"A single small furnace wherein the degrees of heat can be maintained, is sufficient; let it be safely placed where no accident can happen from fire. Put your small glass phial therein, and do not take it out until you see the whole mass converted into a beautiful blood-red colour, the sign of ultimate perfection.

"During the solution, the fire must be gentle, but in the sublimation it must be a little increased, and towards redness, it must be strong.

"During the solution the fire must be soft, in sublimation middling, in the coagulation temperate, in the white-making steady, in the rubyfying strong. If you are ignorant of the heat, you will fail.

"The heat must be linear to the end of the work. When the fire is equally kept, the subject by the action of heat, is better altered from one nature to another, and that which was humid first will become dry, the black will become white, and the white citrine and red.

"When thou seest that the fixt water [secret fire] without any ascending thereof, fret not about the fire; only have patience until the spirit and the body have become one.

"Put it on the fire with such a proportion of heat as shall only excite or stir up the matter, and in a short time that fire [the secret sophic fire] will complete the whole work.

"I swear unto thee, upon the faith of an honest man that if thou urge thy fire so as to make ought sublime in the first regimen, thou wilt destroy the work irrecoverably; be content then to wait forty days and nights [at least], and suffer the tender nature to remain below in the bottom. [Avoiding any kind of sublimation.]

"The heat of the first regimen must be like that of a hen sitting on her eggs, to hatch chickens. . . . This heat continues until blackness, and it may even be continued till the matter is changed into whiteness; but if this heat be transgressed and the matter be kept too hot, you will never obtain the wished for "Raven's Head" [blackness]: but either a sudden transient redness, or a red oily matter may begin to sublime, or swimming upon the superficies. In that case the composition may be taken out of the glass and imbibed anew with our virgin's milk [secret fire] and then you may recommence the concoction with more prudence, endeavouring to avoid similar errors in the future. When the white appears, you may increase your heat a little to the second degree, until the matter be perfectly dried up. [The degree of heat now spoken of is merely comparative. If his winter heat is equal to a hen on her eggs when hatching them, his spring heat must have a proportional increase of temperature. This remark applies equally to what follows.] When the stone is perfectly dry the fire must be increased again.

"Take heed to defend your glass from a violent heat and a sudden cold; make use of a moderate fire and beware of vitrification."

Further warnings about the heat and the glass are included in:

The Marrow of Alchemy by Eirenaeus Philalethes

... beware impatience do not cause thee
Through an itch of mind for to be bold,
In this thy work to transgress Nature's laws
For no man errs sooner through heat or cold
    Than he who through impatience of mind
    Cannot expect its time which he would find

Move not thy glass, nor open, else thou wilt
Endamage, may destroy thy work; beside
Increase not fire rashly, lest that spilt
Thy work thou see. There's nothing all the tide
    That this thy work doth stand so much in fear
    As too much fire: one hour will cost thee dear

Beware thy spirits find not where to exhale,
For that thy work would spill, and also cause
Much hurt to the workman. If you fail
Therein, you break one of the strictest laws
    Of all this work: nor cause them so to rise
    As for to break the glass, which brittle is.

Therefore as strong thy glass be sure thou get
As may be, without either knots or flaws,
Equally blown for strength, which thou shall set
Within a ring of brass, where thou shalt cause
    It to be fixt. ...

142

With gentle fire thy work assay, ...
For that is certain. Be not moved with haste
Thy work to anticipate; no, not a day:
But bide with patience till the black be past,
Then May'st augment thy fire, but not too much,
Rather too little than too great, for such
The Counsel of all the sages old.

But to continue with Bacstrom:

"You need only to prepare the matter. Nature herself alone will perfect it: and if she be not hindered by some contrary thing, she will not overstep her own proper motion, neither in conceiving, nor in generating, nor in bringing forth. Therefore after the preparation of the matter, beware only, lest by too much heat, you make it too hot. Secondly, take heed, lest the spirit should exhale, lest it hurt the operater, also lest it destroy the work, . . . Decoct the composition till it be invested with a most perfect red colour.

"Having prepared your principles, put them, most intimately mixed into a proper glass, so that only one third part of the glass, may be filled. Shut the glass closely that nothing may evaporate. Place it on the fire, and administer the first degree of heat; such a heat that without burning your hand, you may be able to suffer it to rest on the upper part of the neck of the glass. Keep it in this heat without moving or disturbing it until blackness and the various colours appear, and whiteness follows; and until the matter has become snow or silver white and fixed, and the queen is born. After blackness the matter will become dry."

12. Vade Mecum

In the first degree, the stone is called Adrop, philosophical lead, which is not lead, but a supposed derivative of lead, antimony. In the second degree, when the sulphur of Mars has been joined to it, it is called the philosophers' water, and is now their mercury.

Distilled vinegar is not the vinegar of the philosophers. Their most sharp vinegar is another name for the "Secret Fire".

The beginning of this art is only *one* thing; composed of two substances, a fixed Sol and an unfixed mercury. The fixed sol is the seed, and the other remains the Mother, as is called by the adepts. The one is the red fixed servant, and the other is the white wife.

"If you wish to see the sign of putrefaction, it is necessary that you procure an external moving heat, for as nature in the mine boileth by means of a gentle heat, in a like manner, our philosophical matter receives power to alter itself, from such a degree of artificial heat and may be able to stir up its inward power. This artificial heat must not be violent, but soft and gentle, only able to act on the most subtil particles, to raise and mix them, until the whole composition be broken, divided without any manual separation, and converted into perfect blackness."

When commencing experimental work, it is well to be resigned to the fact that nothing will be achieved before twelve months at least, so a settled patience of mind is very necessary. It was however the proud boast of the successful Philalethes that he managed to uncover the whole secret in two and one half years.

The temperatures to be used must be regulated from 150°F. at the commencement to about 250°F. Later the temperature may be higher, but it must be remembered that the compound will itself generate heat as time goes on.

The necessary liquid in the flask, with the correct heat will moisten the contents. Inadequate heat will not initiate this reaction, and too much heat will drive the vapour upwards, leaving the contents dry and hard, which will coalesce into a solid lump, spoiling the experiment. Thus the temperature is most important.

The very first secret uncovered was the nature of the "Secret Fire" which is the mercury of the philosophers, where it is to be found, and how it is to be made, so that it will dissolve the compound of metals into a liquid, exactly as sugar or salt might dissolve in water.

Remember that the alchemist's mercury is not quicksilver or common mercury, for such has no place *whatsoever* in the art of alchemy.

"Mercury" appears everywhere in all the treatises, and is the greatest stumbling block of all, for common mercury will mix with most metals, but will not remain amalgamated with them, as is desired.

Common lead is another metal which the alchemist should never use, but there are derivatives of lead which one *can* use. Lead contains a great deal of dross, which in alchemy is not acceptable.

The augmentation or multiplication of the Stone can be performed in two ways. (1) By repeated solution and coagulation. This coagulation increases the Stone in virtue; (2) By fermentation, which added, then increases the Stone in quantity. The multiplication by fermentation however is soonest accomplished. What has been resolved operates much quicker when fixed by its own ferment, that is gold, or silver (according to which the alchemist desires to produce). The action is similar to leaven: a small quantity leavens the whole lump, and the Stone when projected on imperfect metals transmutes a large quantity into perfect gold.

There are three colours which must of necessity appear in the work, Black, White, and Red. The first two must be produced by a very slow heat, which must be increased very gently.

By way of summary, the following treatise is quite helpful:

ON USE OF MALE AND FEMALE ELEMENTS
RED MAN AND WHITE WIFE

"Decoct the male and female vapour together with the Secret Fire, until such time as they shall become one dry body, for except they be dry, the divers and various colours will not appear. For it will ever be black, while the moisture has the dominion. But if it be once

146

wasted, then it will emit diverse colours, after many and several days.

"And many times it will be changed from colour to colour, till such times as it comes to the fixed whiteness. All the colours of the world will appear in it when the black humidity is dried up. But value none of these colours, for they be not true tincture: yet many times it becomes citrine and reddish, and many times it is dried, and must become liquid again before the whiteness will appear.

[Author's note: All this must have its proper time; one simply cannot hurry it, for, as warned, it is nature's work. Yet the expert might learn in course of experiments how to force things, in the same way as fruit and vegetables are produced before their natural time. Skill must be used, which can only be learnt by experience, with regard to not interfering with the work, and when to interfere, for with so many instructions, one must know when to leave wetness in the flask, and when to dry the matter. Open and shut, dissolve and coagulate, is one of the axioms of the adepts in alchemy, and how can one do this without moving the metals? Working in the dark, that is without knowing whether the work will be spoiled or progressed by manual movement, is a constant problem at first trials.]

"Now while all this is going on the spirit is not joined with the body, nor will it be joined or fixed but in the white colour. Astanus hath said, between the red and the white, all colours will appear, even to the utmost imagination. The cause of these colours is from the extension of the blackness. Therefore as often as any degree or portion of the blackness descends, so often various colours arise until it comes to whiteness. Then it will go on in the same manner to redness.

"Repeat this rubifying three or four times [for however, there must be an addition of new matter—the infant must be fed with his mother's milk or secret fire] and you will have the most perfect red stone, like blood in colour, with which you may tinge mercury and all the imperfect metals into perfect gold."

WHAT IS FERMENTATION
How to Mix our Mercury and Sulphur

"It is necessary that you take of the above red tincture or sulphur three parts, add thereto one part of pure gold, reduced into a subtil calx, and two parts of its water [secret fire]. **Rub** these three together in a clean glass mortar, put it into a strong glass, and in a graduated strong heat, melt it together into a red stone. [The author points at fermentation, but which other artists recommend to be done without adding any secret fire.]

"The 'Fountain' [regulus of antimony and mars] is as it were a mother of the King [gold]. She draws him to her, and killeth him, but the king arises again from death, through her, and unites so firmly with her, that he becomes invulnerable.

"The body of gold must be dissolved, destroyed, putrefied and deprived of all its powers [or natural properties] and this the beginning of the work, assumes first a dark, and later a perfectly black colour called the Raven's Head. This takes place in about forty days. During this blackness the anima of gold is extracted and separated, and is carried aloft and totally separated from the body, the body remaining for some time without life, and like ashes at the bottom of the vessel."

To save much time in research and experiments, and to shorten the time gap before results, it is wise to try more than one experiment at the same time using the same hot-plate, for much depends on the quantity, quality and purity of the metals used.

Use a hot-plate that would be safe to leave working for weeks on end and which has an efficient thermostat, for to stay watching beside the experiment (especially when there is doubt as to the correct procedure) is a heart-breaking business. A housewife preparing food at least knows exactly what to expect and how long the work must take; and the farmer knows the time he must expect to wait before his crops ripen.

To make and prepare the regulus of antimony and iron (which has been called by alchemists silver or Luna or mercury) take four parts antimony, two parts iron, and mix well in powdered form. Then saturate with "Secret Fire", and heat, but only at such a low heat, just to stir up the matter and make it sweat. Wait forty-two to fifty days, by which time the compound should be black. You might try adding one part venus (or copper) to the mixture at the start, but this venus has traditionally been looked down upon with contempt as useless, although one master in alchemy has told us in his treatises that venus must be added. This adept was Eireneaus Philalethes,

148

who wrote many books and claimed he had done the work many times. However the addition of copper is probably a blind.

When the regulus is black, dry off the water and crush it into a fine powder. Of this take three parts and mix in one part Sol in powder. Saturate with Secret Fire, and place into the heat again.

VADE MECUM ON PROJECTION by Philalethes

"When the perfect powder, white or red, is taken out of the philosophical egg, it appears like the most impalpable powder, whose atoms appear more minute if possible than those in the sun's light, and yet it is very ponderous, like burnished gold [or silver]. But when united to or mixed with a perfect body of its own kind, it appears like white or red glass . . . easily pulverizable. . . . The powder in its first state, whether aurific or argentific is too universal or undeterminate—too far above specificated metallic nature [for instant projection] and therefore must be familiarized to metals by mixture with a perfect metallic body. . . . The philosophers advise us to project by gradation till projection ceases; that is to project one part of the tincture on ten parts and again one part of the latter on ten, until after the last projection [no longer glass but] pure gold or silver comes from the fire.

"If in its first state the stone should only go one upon a hundred parts, yet by reiterated solution and coagulations, the energy, penetration and virtue of the tincture may be increased to such a degree that its extent can hardly be calculated.

"If projection is made on mercury, as is mostly done, let the mercury be heated in a crucible, until its crackling noise announces its approaching flight. Then the known quantity of the fermented elixir must be projected on it which enters in an instant and tinges and fixes the mercury. . . . The heat must then be augmented till you perceive the matter in the crucible flow thin and clear. When poured out it will be found to be gold or silver, according to the kind of elixir. . . . The tincture obtained by one continued linear motion, by the first circulation, is called, when perfected, the elixir of bodies. This must be cibated by seven imbibitions, and with the last it must be putrefied, whitened and again congealed and fixed. . . .

"Many working in this art lose their labour by making projection on impure metals . . . but when melted with a perfect metal, of its own species, whereby it is converted into a metallic tinging glass, then and not before, it flows like wax on an imperfect ignited metal, or when thrown on heated mercury. The imperfect metals, being too far removed from perfection, the unfermented tincture does not enter fast enough, not having affinity for the imperfect metals of strength sufficient to separate their scoria in a strong heat. Therefore the powder or tincture gets confusedly mixed and dispersed among the faeces, and the hope of the deluded artist is frustrated."

VADE MECUM ON INCREASE ON POWER & WEIGHT

"I know that many authors do take fermentation in this work for the internal invisible agent, which they call ferment, by whose virtue the fugitive and subtile spirit, without laying on of hands, are of their own accord thickened; and our aforementioned way of fermentation they call cibation with bread and milk [sol and mercury], but I know as well as they, have followed my own judgement in my writings.

"There is then another operation, by which our stone is increased in weight more than virtue. Take of thy sulphur, white or red [this is the completed stone], and to three parts of the sulphur, add a forth of the water [our mercury], and after a little blackness, in six or seven days decoction, thy water newly added shall be increased or thickened, like unto thy sulphur. [Note how the adept does his best to hide his secret, by calling the stone sulphur, and his mercury water.] Then add another fourth part, not in respect of the whole compound, which is now increased a fourth part by the first imbibition, but in reference to thy first sulphur, as thou tookest it at first, which being dried, add another fourth part, and let it be congealed with a convenient fire. Then put in two parts of the water in reference to the three parts of the sulphur, which thou tookest at first, before the first imbibition and in this proportion, imbibe and congeal three other times. At last add five parts of water in the seventh imbibition, still remembering to reckon the water in reference to the sulphur as it was taken at first. [This deliberate manner of writing is done to confuse, and usually succeeds.] Seal thy vessel, and in a fire like to the former, make thy compound pass through all the aforesaid regimens, which will be done in one month, and then thou hast the true stone of the third order; of which one part will fall on a thousand, and tinge perfectly."

150

(All the above was written in one sentence, but has been separated and punctuated as clearly as possible.)

ON MULTIPLICATION OF THE STONE

"To the multiplication of the Stone, is required no labour, save only that thou take the stone, being perfect, and join it with three parts or at the most four parts of mercury of our first work, and govern it with a due fire, in a vessel well closed, so that all the regimens pass with infinite pleasure, and thou shalt have the whole increased a thousand fold beyond what it was before the multiplication of it. And if thou shalt reiterate this work again, in three days thou shalt run through all the regimens, and thy medicine shall be exalted to another millenary virtue of tincture; and if thou shalt yet reiterate the work, it will be perfected in a natural day, and all the regimens shall pass—which will be done afterwards with another reiteration in an hour, nor shalt thou at last be able to find the extent of the virtue of thy stone; it shall be so great that it shall pass thy ingenuity to reckon it, if thou shalt proceed in the work of reiterate multiplication. Now remember to render immortal thanks to God, for thou has now the whole treasure in thy possession."

ON THE MANNER OF PROJECTION

"The manner of Projection is to take of thy stone perfected as it is said, white or red, according to the quality of the medicine, take of either gold or silver four parts, melt them in a clean crucible, then put in of thy stone, white or red, as the metal that is melted is in quality, and being well mixed together in fusion, pour them into an ingot, and thou shalt have a mass which is brittle; take of this mass one part, and mercury well washed ten parts, heat the mercury till it begin to crack, then throw upon it this mixture, which in the twinkling of an eye will pierce; increase thy fire till it be melted, and all will be a medicine of inferior virtue; take then of this, and cast one part upon any metal, purged and melted, to wit, as much as it can tinge, and thou shalt have most pure gold and silver, purer than which nature cannot give. But it is better to make projection gradually until projection cease; for so it will extend farther; for when so little is projected on so much, unless projection be made

151

on mercury, there is a notable loss of the medicine, by reason of the scorias, which do adhere to impure; by how much then the metals are better purged, before projection, by so much more will the matter succeed.

"He who has once, by the blessing of God, perfectly attained this art, I know not what in the world he can wish, but that he may be free from all snares of wicked men, so as to serve God without distraction. But it would be a vain thing, by outward pomp to seek for vulgar applause, such trifles are not esteemed by those who have this art, nay, rather they despise them. He therefore whom God has blessed with this talent, hath this field of content, which far exceeds popular admiration; First if he should live a thousand years, and every day provide for a thousand men, he could not want, for he may increase his stone at his pleasure, both in weight and virtue; so that if a man would, one man that is an adeptist, might transmute into gold and silver that is perfect, all the imperfect metals that are in the whole world; secondly, he may by this art make precious stones and gems, such as cannot be paralleled in nature, for goodness and greatness; thirdly and lastly, he hath a medicine universal, both for prolonging life, and curing all diseases, so that one true adeptist can easily cure all the sick people in the world. I mean his medicine is sufficient."

Now to God Eternal, Immortal and Almighty, be everlasting Praise for these unspeakable gifts, and invaluable treasures.
AMEN.

Appendix I
Paracelsus' Answers

To attempt to present a general overall conception of alchemy, we now quote an important work by Paracelsus, a physician very famous in his day, in which a theory of the art is set forth by question and answer: it is given in an abridged form. This work was written to appeal to the medieval scientific mind, and it is by no means an easy matter for the beginner to appreciate the value of the work, nor will he comprehend how the whole secret is embraced herein in theory; yet it is so. To understand all its implications, the reader is advised to read it though slowly, and after digestion, to read it again. What is not understood at first, will make sense when reverted to subsequently.

THE THEORY OF ALCHEMY by Paracelsus (abridged)

Q. What is the chief study of the philosopher?

A. It is the investigations of the operations of nature.

Q. Whence are all things derived?

A. From one and indivisible nature.

Q. Into how many regions is nature separated?

A. Into four primary regions.

Q. What are they?

A. The dry, the moist, the warm, the cold, which are four elementary qualities, whence all things originate.

Q. How is nature differentiated?

A. Into male and female.

Q. Give a concise definition of nature.

A. It is not visible, though it operates visibly, for it is simply a volatile spirit, fulfilling its office in bodies, and animated by the universal fire which vivifies all things that exist.

Q. What should be the qualities possessed by the examiners of nature?

A. They should be like nature itself. That is to say, they should be truthful, simple, patient, and persevering.

Q. What matters should subsequently engross their attention?

A. The philosophers should most carefully ascertain whether their designs are in harmony with nature, and of a possible and attainable kind. If

153

they would accomplish by their own power anything that is performed usually by the power of nature, they must imitate her in every detail. *ap*

Q. What method must be followed in order to produce something which shall be developed to a superior degree than nature herself develops it? *but not now*

A. The manner of its improvement must be studied, and this is invariably operated by means of a like nature. For example, if it be desired to develop the intrinsic virtue of a given metal beyond its natural condition, the chemist must avail himself of the metallic nature itself, and must be able to discriminate between its male and female differentiations.

Q. Where does the metallic nature store her seeds?

A. In the four elements.

Q. With what materials can the philosopher alone accomplish anything?

A. With the germ of the given matter. This is its elixir or quintessence, more precious by far, and more useful to the artist than is nature herself. Before the philosopher has extracted the seed or germ, nature on his behalf will be ready to perform her duty.

Q. What is the germ or seed of any substance?

A. It is the subtle and perfect decoction and digestion of the subject itself; or rather it is the balm of sulphur, which is identical with the radical moisture of metals.

Q. By what is this seed or germ engendered?

A. By the four elements, earth, water, air, and fire, and through the direct intervention of the imagination of nature.

Q. After what manner do the four elements operate?

A. By means of an incessant and uniform motion; each one according to its quality, depositing its seed in the centre of the earth, where it is subjected to digestion and action, and is subsequently expelled in an upward direction by the laws of movement.

Q. What do the philosophers understand by the centre of the earth?

A. A certain void place where nothing may repose, and the existence of which is assumed.

Q. When then do the four elements expel and deposit their seeds?

A. In the ex-centre, or in the margin or circumference of the centre, which after it has appropriated a portion, casts out the surplus, into the region of excrement, scoria, fire and formless chaos.

Q. Illustrate this teaching by example.

A. Take any level table and set in its centre a vase filled with water; surround the vase with several things of different colours; especially salt, taking care that a proper distance intervenes between them all. Then pour out the water from the vase, and it will flow in streams

154

here and there; one will encounter a substance of a red colour, and will assume of red; another will pass over the salt and will contract a saline flavour; for it is certain that water does not modify the places which it traverses, but the diverse characteristics of places change the nature of water. In the same way the seed which is deposited by the four elements at the centre of the earth, is subject to a variety of modifications in the places through which it passes; so that every existing substance is produced in the likeness of its channel, and when on its arrival at a certain point encounters pure earth and water, a pure substance results, but the contrary in an opposite case.

Q. After what manner do the elements procreate this seed?

A. In order to the complete elucidation of this point, it must be observed that there are two gross elements that are heavy, and two that are volatile in character. Two in a like manner are dry, and two humid, one of the four being actually excessively dry. There are also masculine and feminine. Now each of them has a marked tendency to reproduce its own species within its own sphere. Moreover they are never in repose, but are perpetually interacting, and each of them separates, of and by itself, the most subtle portion thereof. Their general place of meeting is in the centre, where coming to mix their seeds, they agitate and finally expel them to the exterior.

Q. What is the true and first matter of all metals?

A. The first matter, properly so called, is dual in its essence, or is in itself of a twofold nature. One nevertheless cannot create a metal without the concurrence of the other. The first and the palmary essence is an aerial humidity, blended with a warm air, in the form of a fatty water, which adheres to all substances indiscriminately whether they pure or impure.

Q. How has this humidity been named by the philosophers.

A. Mercury.

Q. By what is it governed?

A. By the rays of the sun and the moon.

Q. What is the second matter?

A. The warmth of the earth, otherwise that dry heat which is termed sulphur by the philosophers.

Q. What therefore should be done?

A. The matter must be effectively separated from its impurities, for there is no metal how pure soever, which is entirely freed from imperfections, though their extent varies. Now all superfluities, cortises, and scoria must be peeled off, and purged from out of the matter in order to discover its seed.

Q. What should receive the most careful attention of the philosophers?

A. Assuredly the end of nature, and this is to be by no means looked for in the vulgar metals, because these having issued already from the hands of the fashioner, it is no longer to be found there.

Q. For what precise reason?

A. Because the vulgar metals and chiefly gold, are absolutely dead, while ours on the contrary, are absolutely living and possess a soul.

Q. What is the life of metals?

A. It is no other substance than fire, when they are as yet embedded in the mines.

Q. What is their death?

A. Their life and death are in reality one principle, for they die as they live, by fire; but their death is by a fire of fusion.

Q. After what manner are metals conceived in the womb of the earth?

A. When the four elements have developed their power or virtue in the centre of the earth, and have deposited their seed; nature in the course of a distillatory process, sublimes them superficially by the warmth and energy of perpetual movement.

Q. Into what does the air resolve itself when it is distilled through the pores of the earth?

A. It resolves itself into water from which all things spring.

Q. In this state it is merely a humid vapour, out of which there is subsequently evolved the principle of all substances.

Q. Are Saturn, Jupiter, Mars, and Venus, the Sun and Moon separately endowed with individual seed?

A. One is common to them all; their differences are to be accounted for by the locality from which they are derived, not to speak of the fact that natures completes her work with far greater rapidity in the procreation of silver, than in that of gold; and so of the other metals each in its own proportion.

Q. How is gold formed in the bowels of the earth?

A. When this vapour of which we have spoken is sublimed in the centre of the earth, and when it has passed through warm and pure places, where a warm and sulphureous grease adheres to the channels, then this vapour which the philosophers have denominated their mercury, becomes adapted and joined to the grease, which it sublimes with itself; from such amalgamation there is produced a certain unctuousness, which abandoning the vapourous form assumes that of grease, and is sublimed in other places which have been cleansed by the preceding vapour, and the earth thereof has consequently been rendered more subtle, pure and humid; it fills the pores of the earth, is joined thereto, and gold is produced as a result.

Q. How is Saturn engendered?

A. It occurs when the said unctuosity or grease, passed through places which are totally impure and cold.

Q. How is Venus brought forth?

A. She is produced in localities where the earth is pure, but is mingled with impure sulphur.

Q. What power does the vapour which we have recently mentioned possess in the centre of the earth?

A. By its continual progress it has the power of perpetually rarifying what is crude and impure, and of successfully attracting to itself all that is pure around it.

Q. How is the generation of seed comprised in the metallic kingdom?

A. By the artifice of nature; the four elements in the first generation of nature, distill a ponderous vapour of water into the centre of the earth; and this is the seed of metals and it is called mercury; not on account of its essence, but because of its fluidity, and the facility with which it adheres to everything.

Q. Why is this vapour compared to sulphur?

A. Because of its internal heat.

Q. From what species of mercury are we to conclude that the metals are composed?

A. This refers exclusively to the mercury of the philosophers; and in no sense the common or vulgar mercury, which cannot become a seed, seeing that like other metals, it contains its own seed.

Q. What therefore must actually be accepted as the subject of our art of alchemy?

A. The seed alone, otherwise the fixed grain, and not the whole body which is turned into sulphur, or living male; or into mercury or living female.

Q. What operation must afterwards be performed?

A. They must be joined together so that they may form a germ, after they proceed to the procreation of a fruit which conforms to their nature.

Q. What is the part of the artist in this operation?

A. The artist must do nothing but separate that which is subtle from that which is gross.

Q. To what therefore is the whole philosophic combination reduced?

A. The development of one into two, and the reduction of two into one and nothing further.

Q. Whither must we turn for the seed and life of metals and minerals?

A. The seed of minerals is properly the water which exists in the centre and heart of the minerals.

Q. How does nature operate by the help of art?

A. Every seed, whatsoever its kind is useless, unless by nature or art it is placed in a suitable matrix, where it receives its life by the coction of the germ, and by congealation of the pure grain.

Q. How is the seed subsequently nourished and preserved?

A. By the warmth of its body.

Q. What is therefore performed by art in the mineral kingdom?

A. He finishes what cannot be finished by nature, on account of the crudity of the air, permeating the pores of all bodies on the surface, but not in the bowels of the earth.

Q. What correspondence have the metals among themselves?

A. The sun enters into all, but it is never ameliorated by its inferiors.

Q. What is the object of research among the philosophers?

A. Proficiency in the art of perfecting what nature has left imperfect in the mineral kingdom, and the attainment of the treasure of the Philosophers' Stone.

Q. What is this stone?

A. The stone is nothing else than the radical humidity of the elements, perfectly purified and educed into a sovereign fixation, which causes it to perform such great things for health; the life being resident exclusively in the humid radical.

Q. In what does the secret of accomplishing this admirable work consist?

A. It consists in knowing how to educe from potentiality into activity the innate warmth, or fire of nature, which is enclosed in the radical humidity.

Q. Why does this medicine heal every species of disease?

A. It is simply because it powerfully fortifies the natural warmth which it gently stimulates, while other physics irritate it by too violent an action.

Q. How can you demonstrate to me the truth of the art in the matter of the tincture?

A. Firstly the truth is founded on the fact that the physical powder being composed of the same substance of the metals, namely quicksilver, has the faculty of combining with these in fusion, one nature easily embracing another which is like itself. Secondly seeing that the imperfection of the base metals is owing to the crudeness of their quicksilver, and to that alone, the physical powder which is a ripe and decocted quicksilver, and in itself a pure fire, can easily communicate to them its own maturity, and can transmute them into its nature, after it has attracted their crude humidity, that is to say, their quicksilver, which is the sole substance which transmute them, the rest being nothing but scoria and excrements, which are rejected in projection.

Q. What road should the philosopher follow that he may attain to the knowledge and execution of the physical work?

158

A. By observing how the chaos in the creation of the world was evolved.

Q. What was the matter of the chaos?

A. It could be nothing else but a humid vapour, because water alone enters into all created substances, which all finish in a strange term, this term being a proper subject for the impression of all forms.

Q. What profit may the philosopher derive from these considerations, and what should he especially remark in the method of creation which was pursued by the Supreme Being?

A. In the first place, he should observe the matter out of which the world was made; he will see that out of this confused mass, the Sovereign artist began by extracting light, that this light in the same moment dissolved the darkness which covered the face of the earth, and that it served as the universal form of the matter. He will then easily perceive that in the generation of all composite substances, a species of irradiation takes place, and the separation of light and darkness, wherein Nature is an undeviating copyist of the Creator. The philosopher will equally understand after what manner, by the action of this light, the empyrean or firmament which divides the inferior and the superior waters was subsequently produced; how the sky was studded with luminous bodies; and how the necessity for the moon arose, which owing to the space intervening between the things above and the things below; for the moon is an intermediate torch between the superior worlds and the inferior worlds, receiving the celestial influences and communicating them to the earth. Finally he will understand how the Creator, in the gathering of the waters produced dry land.

Q. What kind of mercury must the Artificer take to make use of in performing the work?

A. Of a mercury which as such, is not found on the earth, but is taken from bodies; yet not from vulgar mercury, as it has been falsely said.

Q. As you have told me that mercury is the one thing which the philosopher must understand, will you give me a description of it to avoid misconception?

A. In respect of its nature, mercury is dual; that is our mercury is fixed and volatile. In regard to its motion, it is also dual, for it has a motion of ascent and descent. By that of descent, this is its first office previous to congealation. By its ascentional movement, it rises seeking to be purified, and as this is after congealation, it is considered to be the radical moisture of metals, which beneath its vile scoria, still preserves the nobility of its first origin.

Q. Why is the vulgar mercury unfitted to the needs of the work?

A. Because the wise artist must take notice that vulgar mercury has an insufficient quantity of sulphur, and he should consequently operate upon a body created by nature, in which nature herself has united the sulphur and mercury that it is the work of the artist to separate.

Q. What must he subsequently do?

A. He must purify them and join them anew together.

Q. How many species of mercury are there known to the philosophers?

A. Mercury may be regarded under four aspects. The first is called the seed; the second is the mercury of Nature; which is the bath or vase of the philosophers; otherwise the humid radical. To the third has been applied the designation of the mercury of the philosophers because it is found in their laboratory and in their minera. It is in the sphere of Saturn; it is the Diana of the Wise, it is the true salt of metals, after the acquisition of which the true philosophic work may be truly said to have begun. In its fourth aspect, it is called common mercury, which yet is not that of the vulgar, but rather properly the true air of the philosophers, the true middle substance of water, the true secret and concealed fire, called also the common fire, because it is common to all minerals and metals; and thence do they derive their quality and quantity.

Q. When may the philosopher venture to undertake the work?

A. When he is, theoretically able to extract by means of a crude spirit, a digested spirit out of a body in dissolution, which digested spirit he must again rejoin to the vital oil.

Q. Explain to me this theory in a clearer manner?

A. It may be demonstrated more clearly in the actual process. The great experiment may be undertaken when the philosopher by means of a vegetable menstruum, with which menstruum united he must wash the earth, and then exalt it into a celestial quintessence, to compose the sulphurous thunderbolt which instantaneously penetrates the substances.

Q. Have those persons a proper acquaintance with nature, who pretend to make use of vulgar gold for seed, and of vulgar mercury for the dissolvent, or the earth in which it should be sown?

A. Assuredly not, because neither the one nor the other possess the external agent.

Q. In seeking the auriferous seed elsewhere than in gold itself, is there no danger of producing a species of monster, since one appears to be parting from nature?

A. It is undoubtedly true that in gold is contained the auriferous seed, and that in more perfect condition than is found in any other body; but this does not force us to make use of vulgar gold, for such a seed

160

is equally found in each of the other metals, and in nothing else but that fixed grain which nature has infused in the first congealation of mercury, all metals having one origin and a common substance, as will ultimately be unveiled to those who are worthy by application and assiduous study.

Q. What follows from this doctrine?

A. It follows that although the seed is more perfect in gold, it may be extracted much more easily from another body than gold itself, other bodies being more open, that is to say less digested and less restricted in their humidity.

Q. Give me an example taken from nature?

A. Vulgar gold may be likened to a fruit which having come to a perfect maturity, has been cut off from the tree, although it contains a most perfect and digested seed; notwithstanding should anyone set it in the ground with a view to its multiplication, much time, trouble and attention will be consumed in the development of its vegetative capabilities. On the other hand if a cutting or root be taken from the same tree, and similarly planted, in a short time with no trouble, it will spring and produce much fruit.

Q. How does nature deposit metals in the bowels of the earth?

A. Nature manufactures them all from sulphur and mercury, and forms them from their double vapour.

Q. What do you mean by this double vapour? How can metals be formed thereby?

A. In order to a complete understanding to this question, it must first be stated that mercurial vapour is united to a sulphureous vapour in a cavernous place which contains a saline water which serves as their matrix. Thus is formed firstly the vitriol of nature; secondly by the commotion of the elements, there is developed out of this vitriol of nature a new vapour, which is neither mercurial nor sulphureous, yet allied to both these natures, and this passing through places to which the grease of sulphur adheres, is joined therewith, and out of their union a glutinous substance is produced, otherwise a formless mess, which is permeated with the vapour which fills these cavernous places. By this vapour acting through the sulphur it contains, are produced the perfect metals, provided the locality and the vapour are pure. If the locality and the vapour are impure, imperfect metals result. The terms perfection and imperfection have reference to various degrees of concoction,

Q. What is actually the living gold of the philosophers?

A. It is exclusively the fire of mercury, or that ingeneous virtue, contained in the radical moisture, to which it has already communicated

161

the fixity and the nature of sulphur, whence it has emanated, the mercurial character of the whole substance of philosophical sulphur permitting it to be alternately termed sulphur.

Q. What other name is also given to the living gold by the adepts?

A. They also term it their living sulphur, and their true fire. They recognise its existence in all bodies, and there is nothing that can subsist without it.

Q. Where must we look for our living gold, our living mercury, and our true fire?

A. In the house of mercury.

Q. By what is this fire nourished?

A. By the air.

Q. What should be done by the philosopher after he has extracted his mercury?

A. He should develop it from potentiality into activity.

Q. Cannot nature perform this of herself?

A. No; because she stops short after the first sublimation, and out of the matter which is thus disposed, do the metals engender.

Q. What do the philosophers understand by their gold and silver?

A. The philosophers apply to their sulphur the name of gold, and to their mercury the name of silver.

Q. Whence are they derived?

A. I have already stated that they are derived from a homogeneous body wherein they are found in great abundance, whence also they know how to extract both by an admirable process.

Q. When this operation has been duly formed, to what other point of the practice must they next apply themselves?

A. To the confection of the philosophical amalgam which must be done with great care, but can only be accomplished after the preparation and sublimation of the mercury.

Q. When should your matter be combined with the living gold?

A. During the period of amalgamation only, and thenceforth there is one substance; the process is shortened by the addition of sulphur, while the tincture is at the same time augmented.

Q. What is contained in the centre of the radical moisture?

A. It contains and conceals sulphur, which is covered with a hard rind.

Q. What must be done to apply it to the great work?

A. It must be drawn out of its bonds with consummate skill, and by the method of putrefaction.

Q. Does nature in her work in the mines, possess a menstruum which is adapted to the dissolution and liberation of the sulphur.

A. No, because there is no local movement. Could nature unassisted

162

provide us with the physical stone, which is sulphur exalted and increased in virtue, there would be no need of the alchemical art.

Q. Can you elucidate this doctrine by an example?

A. By an enlargement of the previous comparison of a fruit or seed, which in the first place is put into the earth for its solution, and afterwards for its multiplication. Now, the philosopher who is in a position to discern what is good seed, extracts it from its centre and consigns it to its proper earth, when it has been well cured and prepared, and therein he rarifies it in such a manner that its prolific virtue is increased and multiplied.

Q. In what does the whole secret of the seed consist?

A. In the knowledge of its proper earth.

Q. What do you understand by the seed in the work?

A. I understand the interior heat, or the specific spirit, which is enclosed in the humid radical, which in other words is the middle substance of living silver, the proper sperm of metals which contains its own seed.

Q. How do you set free the sulphur from its bonds?

A. By putrefaction.

Q. What pains must be taken by the philosopher to extract that which he requires?

A. He must take great pains to eliminate the fetid vapours and impure sulphurs, after which the seed must be injected.

Q. By what indication may the artist be assured that he is in the right road at the beginning.

A. When he finds that the dissolvent and the thing dissolved are converted into one form and one matter at the period of dissolution.

Q. How many solutions or processes do you count in the great work?

A. There are three. The first solution is that which reduces the crude metallic body into its elements of sulphur and silver; the second is that of the physical body, and the third is the solution of the mineral earth.

Q. How is the metallic body reduced by the first solution into sulphur and then into mercury?

A. By the secret artificial fire which is the burning star.

Q. How is this operation performed?

A. By extracting from the subject in the first place, the mercury or the vapour of the elements, and after purification by using it to liberate the sulphur from its bonds by corruption, of which blackness is the indication.

Q. How is the second solution performed?

A. When the physical body is resolved into the two substances previously mentioned, and has acquired the celestial nature.

163

Q. What is the name which applied by the philosophers to the matter during this period?

A. It is called the physical chaos, and it is in fact the true first matter, a name which can hardly be applied before the conjunction of the male, which is sulphur, and the female which is salt or mercury.

Q. To what does the third solution refer?

A. It is the humectation of the mineral earth, and it is closely bound up with multiplication.

Q. What fire must be made use of in our work?

A. That fire which is used by nature.

Q. What is the potency of this fire?

A. It dissolved everything that is in the world, because it is the principle of all dissolution and corruption.

Q. Why is it also termed mercury?

A. Because it is in its nature aerial, and a most subtle vapour, which partaked at the same time of sulphur, whence it has contracted some contamination.

Q. Where is this fire concealed?

A. It is concealed in the subject of our art.

Q. Who is it that is familiar with and can produce this fire?

A. It is known to the wise who can produce and purify it.

Q. What is the essential potency and characteristic of this fire?

A. It is excessively dry, and is continually in motion; it seeks to disintegrate and to educe things from potentiality to actuality; it is in a word, that which coming upon solid places, circulated in a vapourous form upon the matter, and dissolves it.

Q. How may this fire be most easily distinguished?

A. By the sulphureous excrements in which it is developed, and by the saline envirement in which it is clothed.

Q. What must be added to this fire so as to accentuate its capacity for incineration in the feminine species?

A. On account of its extreme dryness, it requires to be moistened.

Q. How many philosophical fires do you enumerate?

A. There are in all three; the natural, unnatural, and the contranatural.

Q. Explain to me these three species of fires?

A. The natural fire is the masculine fire, or chief agent; the unnatural fire is the feminine; which is the dissolvent of nature, nourishing a white smoke, and assuming that form. This smoke is quickly dissipated unless much care be exercised, and it is almost incombustible, though by sublimation it becomes corporeal and resplendent. The contranatural fire is that which disintegrates the compound, and has the power to unbind what has been bound very closely by nature.

Q. Where is our matter to be found?

A. It must be specially sought for in the metallic nature, where it is more easily available, than elsewhere.

Q. What kind must be preferred before all others?

A. The most mature, the most appropriate, and the easiest; but before all things, care must be taken that the metallic essence shall be present, not only potentially, but actually, and that there is moreover a metallic splendour.

Q. Is everything contained in this subject?

A. Yes, but nature at the same time must be assisted, so that the work may be perfected and hastened, by means which are familiar to the higher grades of the experiment.

Q. Is this subject exceedingly precious?

A. It is vile and originally without native elegance. Fundamentally it is not saleable because it is useful in our work alone.

Q. What does our matter contain?

A. It contains salt, sulphur and mercury.

Q. What operation is it most important to be able to perform?

A. The successive extraction of salt, sulphur and mercury.

Q. How is that done?

A. By sole and perfect sublimation.

Q. What is in the first place extracted?

A. Mercury in the form of a white smoke.

Q. What follows? Igneous water and sulphur.

Q. What then?

A. Dissolution with purified salt; in the first place volatalising that which is fixed, and afterwards fixing that which is volatile. This into a precious earth which is the vase of the philosophers, and is wholly perfect.

As the questions and answers have continued in the above work, the questions have become more pertinent and interesting, and the answers ever more tantalising; yet time and a deeper knowledge will show that every answer is to the point, and true.

165

Appendix II

Equipment and Materials Required for the First Operation of Alchemy

1. The most important piece of equipment is the hot-plate. In times past the alchemists only had primitive fires or ovens that were kept going with all kinds of fuels that needed constant watching to prevent them going cold, for periods of time often measured in months. Any diminution in heat could result in failure of the experiment, thus wasting months of work. Now, thermostatically controlled hot-plates, with adjustable temperatures which will keep going for weeks, months, or years without supervision, are available to the researcher. A hot-plate of approximately 18 by 10 in. will allow several experiments to be run at the same temperature at the same time.

2. At least four Pyrex flasks of 150 ml and two of 250 ml to act as receiving flasks for the condensed vapour rising from the retort containing the metals. This is the philosopher's mercury which is extracted from the powdered metals with a heat which must not exceed 150–170°F.

3. Two retorts of 100 ml and one of 250 ml, with long necks, made of Pyrex to withstand the constant heat. These must be flat-bottomed to stand firmly on the hot-plate.

4. A home-made surround of thick asbestos, with cardboard or asbestos cover, to conserve the heat generated by the hot-plate. This should have fairly tight apertures for the necks of the retorts to protrude through.

5. The ground-glass bungs with which the retorts are fitted should be replaced by rubber bungs, as these will merely blow out if too much pressure is generated in the retort rather than causing the apparatus to explode, with the consequent loss of equipment, time and metals. There should be a number of replacement bungs, as the rubber tends to harden in the heat. However be very careful not to allow vapour to be lost, and therefore do not open the retorts too often; after all, the farmer does not pull up his seeds every now and then to see how they are getting along. Make sure that all closures are absolutely airtight.

6. A range of Kilner jars to store various materials and products of the work under airtight conditions, able to withstand heat.

7. Accurate scales graduated in sixteenths of an ounce, up to a pound.

8. Pestle and mortar for crushing compounds hardened under heat.

9. A small strong magnet, for iron filings.

10. A few plastic funnels with spouts capable of entering the retorts.
11. Stirrers and spoons, to remove matter from the flasks.
12. Various grade mesh sieves.
13. Brushes for manipulating fine powders.
14. A small torch to inspect the retorts during the heating.
15. Evaporating dishes to dry metals.
16. Most importantly, a notebook to record dates, results and quantities.

The metals to be used

All metals used in alchemy should be in powder form, so as to obtain the most intimate mixtures without the necessity of fusion. These may be obtained from manufacturers, but it is important that they be as chemically pure (99 per cent) and as finely ground as possible, as this will save much time.

a. Sol or Gold *or* Luna or Silver   1 part
   (Never to be used together at any stage)

added to

b. Antimony
   with Mars or Iron in a regulus   1 part

and

c. Venus or Copper (if it is decided to use it)   1 part
(Venus is a blind, and is often referred to with contempt by the alchemists, but see Chapter 6 for details of this difficulty.)

Appendix III

Signs and Symbols used in Alchemical Literature

⊙ Sol. Gold. Sun.
☽ Luna. Silver. Moon. Regulus of Antimony and Mars.
♂ Mars. Iron.
♀ Venus. Copper.
♄ Saturn. Lead. Antimony.
♃ Jupiter. Tin.
☿ Mercury. Quicksilver.
♁ Sulphur. Earth, drawn from all metals.
▽̵ Earth. Metals generally.
▽ Water. Not ordinary water but philosophic mercury.
△ Fire. Heat or Sophic Fire.
△̵ Air. Vapour.
⊖ Salt. Part of the nature of metals, not common salt.
℥ Retort, used in distillation.

Glossary

AIR: Vapour, not the atmosphere. The vapour arising from metals.

ALKAHEST: Secret fire.

AMALGAM: Mixture of metals by fusion.

ARGENT VIVE: Philosopher's mercury or "living silver".

ATHANOR: Oven used by the alchemists, now superseded.

AURUM ALBUM: White gold.

AZOTH: First mixture of metals.

BALNEUM MARIAE: A warm water bath kept at a temperature bearable by a human being.

CALCINATION: To reduce by heat but not by burning.

CIBATION: The wetting of the dried matter.

COLOUR SEQUENCE: Jet black, white, citrine, blood red.

CONGEALATION: Solidification from liquid.

CONJUNCTION: Amalgamation of several elements.

CUPELLATION: The metallurgical test for assaying gold, first mentioned by Gerber.

DIGESTION: Concoction for the purpose of extracting the essence from a substance.

DISSOLUTION: The slow separation of a body into its components in a liquid.

EARTH: Metals are often referred to as "earth".

EXALTATION: Raising the power or virtue of the philosophers' stone to enable it to transmute.

FERMENTATION: Adding the required precious metal as a "yeast" to the philosophers' stone enabling it to transmute base metals into this particular precious metal.

JUPITER: Planetary name for tin.

LAPIS PHILOSOPHORUM: The philosophers' stone, which is of course a powder and not a stone.

LUNA: The planetary name for silver, often referring to the regulus of antimony and iron.

MAGNESIA: Sometimes used for loadstone or talc, but by many alchemists merely applied to mixtures of metals.

MARS: Planetary name for iron.

170

Glossary

MENSTRUUM: Any fluid that dissolves a solid, sometimes a catalyst.

MERCURIAL SUBLIMATE: Vapour of metals, not used by the alchemists in its modern chemical meaning.

MERCURY, philosophical: Sophic fire, a brilliant clear liquid, not ordinary mercury.

MERCURY, vulgar: Common quicksilver.

MULTIPLICATION: Increasing the quality and quantity of the Philosophers' Stone.

OUR FIRE: Secret fire.

PEACOCK'S TAIL: The varied colours that arise during the course of the work which resemble the colours seen when petrol is spilt on a wet surface.

PHILOSOPHERS' STONE: The powder with which the transmutation is finally effected.

PHILOSOPHICAL VITRIOL: Not aqua regis, associated with copper or the vapour extracted from copper.

PROJECTION: The final work of transmutation into gold or silver.

PUTREFACTION: The first change to be seen, the appearance of blackness.

REBIS: Two metals joined like a regulus with the aid of a catalyst.

RED MAN: Iron, or occasionally gold, or copper.

REGULUS: Two metals mixed in a natural manner, but not by the application of ordinary fire but by a natural heat bearable by man.

SALT: Not ordinary salt, but part of the nature of metals.

SATURN: Planetary name for lead, but to the alchemists this quite often referred to a black stage rather than the metal lead.

SECRET FIRE: See philosophical mercury.

SEPARATION: To break up into light and heavy parts.

SOL: Gold.

SOPHIC FIRE: See philosophical mercury.

SOPHIC MERCURY: See philosophical mercury.

SUBLIMATION: Extraction by volatilisation or distillation.

SULPHUR, philosophers': That which is extracted from metals which the alchemists claim was present in all metals in varying quantities, not chemical sulphur.

TRANSMUTATION: The changing of one metal into another.

UNIVERSAL MENSTRUUM: See philosophical mercury.

VENUS: Planetary name for copper.

WATER: Refers to philosophers' mercury.

WHITE WIFE: A white metal sometimes antimony.

Bibliography

In this book, complete treatises, extracts and quotations are taken from the following books written by masters of the art of alchemy, mainly from the Middle Ages. Fitted together, these produce a picture that will clarify much that has never been generally known about alchemy. Nevertheless, a warning is here given that the serious student should be on guard when reading any of the undermentioned books and not accept everything he finds as true. Most of these books may be found by readers in the library of the British Museum. Though there are many thousands of alchemical treatises spread around the world, the following are recommended as the most practical.

Ali-Puli, *Epistles*, 1951.

Anonymous German Alchemist, *Hermetic Triumpth*, 1723.

Artephius, *Secret Book*, 1624.

Bacon, Roger, *Root of the World* (*Radix Mundi*), 1692.

Hamilton-Jones, J. W., *Bacstrom's Alchemical Anthology*, 1960.

Hermes Trismegistus, *The Golden Treatise*, 1692.

Kelley, Edward, "Book of St. Dunstans" (in *Alchemical Writings*, 1893).

Maier, Michael, *Atalanta Fugiens*, 1617.

Paracelsus, "Theory of Alchemy" (in *Works*, 1894).

Philalethes, Eirenaeus, *Marrow of Alchemy*, 1654.
   Ripley Revived, 1678.

Pontanus, John, *Sophic Fire*, 1624.

Ripley, George, "Twelve Gates" (in *Opera Omnia Chemica*, 1649).

Sendivogius, Michael, *A New Light of Alchemy*, 1650.

Synesius, "The True Book" (in Basil Valentine's *Triumphant Chariot of Antimony*, 1678).

Urbigerus, Baro, *One Hundred Aphorisms*, 1690.

Vaughan, Thomas (Eugenius Philalethes), *Magical and Alchemical Writings* (ed. A. E. Waite, 1888).

Index

173

Index

175

Index